I0697908

Politics by the Ball

by Marlon C. Manning

RoseDog Books
PITTSBURGH, PENNSYLVANIA 15238

The contents of this work including, but not limited to, the accuracy of events, people, and places depicted; opinions expressed; permission to use previously published materials included; and any advice given or actions advocated are solely the responsibility of the author, who assumes all liability for said work and indemnifies the publisher against any claims stemming from publication of the work.

All Rights Reserved
Copyright © 2019 by Marlon C. Manning

No part of this book may be reproduced or transmitted, downloaded, distributed, reverse engineered, or stored in or introduced into any information storage and retrieval system, in any form or by any means, including photocopying and recording, whether electronic or mechanical, now known or hereinafter invented without permission in writing from the publisher.

RoseDog Books
585 Alpha Drive
Suite 103
Pittsburgh, PA 15238
Visit our website at www.rosedogbookstore.com

ISBN: 978-1-6442-6740-0
eISBN: 978-1-6442-6763-9

There can be no legitimate systems of working government, without a large majority of percentile support coming from the people. A support which is migratory in feelings perhaps. Which evolves in the person from internal and external senses. These are the people who take a stake in valuing themselves as American, and their place in the history of the United States. Through fully participating, and supporting their right to exercise public freedoms or referendum voting rights. For appointment of valued leadership, or to create legal legislation which matters to the people of the United States. An enjoying the rights given to people through perceived visions of the writers of the Declaration Of Independence, and the U.S. Constitution. Which tradition is now carried on through state legislators or congressional members who create proposed bills, and make referendum votes to create laws. Although many people in our world argue that freedom doesn't come without struggle! It is still largely believed by some people that civil rights, and voting has been used in America as a deception. And that the real system of governmental operations is comprised for a certain class of people, race, oligarchs, businessmen, and politicians. Under hinged from surface view but operating. However, the fact remains that if you live in a developed country. Abroad or in the United States, such countries who make the bold attempt to establish organized institutions of governmental systems. Or simply maintaining the current systems put in place. In my view, must have a people with certain characteristic traits. This lies within a people or mankind who possess the proper aim & life purpose. As a natural part of peoples' everyday active societal behavior. Not something made up or experimental. It virtually becomes impossible to establish a firm foundational base for creating a governmental system. Without an established people to build on evolved branches of knowledge which come through them in the form of effective leadership establishments. For many people, political science in our modern day is associated with political party affiliations, their existing political ideology, lobbyists, congressional debates, and social event happenings in our society which effect political debate. Included are politicized cultures through media outlets, or social forums created to galvanize people for discussion of issues which effect our public social system. Which ultimately has effects at times, on the social-behavioral action of politicians, and the manner by which they choose to legislate. Or impose their will on our world. No matter if you're an elected politician or see yourself at the grassroots level. Supporting issues which may be important to you, an organization, race, culture, or a broader group. At times people who possess the political ball, republicans, democrats. Attempt to reframe changes through their analysis of the action scope of power in political activities. Which have an impact on domestic life within America and around the world. The early establishment of the 13 colonies was a model of united geographical areas as a formed system of government. Through peoples' belief in their own human stabilization, and a reforming of policies that they no longer believed in that had existing effects on their social life. Otherwise, there would have never been a need to escape the old world of King James to come to a new world for establishment of a specific type of colony. Yet, as time would move forward people seen a need for a broadening system of government which they hoped would regulate the needs of all people. From this need grassroots work persisted, the

Declaration OF Independence emerged, Constitution, and first polit-ical parties would emerge but not without fights or struggle. An the quest to form a United States would persist. In what the people viewed as a new world. True that the aim & purpose of Hamilton, Jefferson, and founding fathers' in comparison to our modern civilization has changed. Evident through reformed political policy that has changed the scope of portions of federal legislation through the voting rights bill. However, in this 21st century one sounding consensus from the people of many varying social backgrounds, would agree that intricate parts of the American governmental systems need reform. This has be-come apparent through peoples' expressive actions in our public society. Which expresses a more common character of evil. That is an indica-tion of non-caring attitudes about the lifes' or rights of other people. Which is a descent from systematic organization, respect for individ-uals' rights, and governmental law. Which some people and political actions as well, could be associated with psycho-pathic behaviors. Such a statement says that our government as a whole must re-assess. Is our government following suit? Having similar characteristic action expres-sions similar to people who commit acts within our public view, but to-wards people who live in public or abroad? Or does American politics as of late, simply fail to answer the call of what is good for mankind alike? If so, that means that politics is completely occupied with a full agenda, with no real sense of its' own character, aim or purpose. Pos-sibly heading towards self-destruction without clinical intervention per-haps? Or having understanding for the need of creating Bi-partisan consensus character for reform of our legal social systems. However, the overall analysis of political activity and the social behavior that it produces in many people, suggest that worldly systems of government have become more volatile. Or more commonly prone to make critical errors. While political science is now being used as an ideological play thing among political parties when they possess the ball in Washington D.C. As globalization sovereignty persist through aggressive education, war, diplomacy, trade, and technological advancements which allow people from other countries to see every day America. A new societal behavior has been spawning domestically and abroad. Producing a new critique analysis of political activity in America, mood change behavior towards our existing systems of government, and our people. New generations of people may begin to take on a different view of the United States Of America. As an established country with a proven record of working system of government, our people, and our legitimacy as leaders to other nations. This book is written for students of political science who analyze America's association with issues in a world that is changing globally. As a means of producing accurate written analysis of political activity, actions, and behaviors associated with people in our world. Most importantly, the impact their actions have on the laws they create and the impact on our public social life in America.

To The Student

Those who have an interest in the many issues associated with politics. Should see political science as knowledge that deals specifically with forming systems of government, the peoples' impact on the law through their public social behavior, and the creation of formative analysis of political activity. Moreover, I would like to offer some suggestions on how to approach this text. As each student reads, always have paper, and pencil available. Refer to theory, written material within the book, or from research to create a base foundational means for creating your own political science analysis. However, it is pertinent that you engage this text as an active reader who takes notes. To develop a perception for the presented critique analysis. This text serves as a workbook to inspire students to engage as people who care about their political social life within formed systems of government. With the hope that you have a more active behavioral role in political activity that shapes America, and our world.

Contents

Theory

Separation Of Powers Is Societal Segregation

Chapter One

Political Science History

There are many tangible issues that a person's hand can gently grab onto from the branch leaves of a political science history tree. Explore their outer & internal makeup, sort of like leaves from any good date or fruit tree, but without pulling them off completely. A good farmer can scientifically cultivate in this manner without killing parts of a crop he has planted. This analogy is used in creating a healthy debate which inspects, and explores the direction of the United States Of America. An the issues which impact the social politics of many people around the world. While understanding that if you're a person who has followed current event happenings in the life of the American political tree, that some issues are DEAD! What has happened to American political cultivation? We could agree that it's true, that the manner in which nature sets its' foundational base, that the directional course for the future remains set. At the outset, American social life had been driven by a type of mankind with Aim & Purpose for political cultivation in the society. With a large consensus support for the peoples' direction. My point, is that the effort was together. Not a separatist type of effort. However, what has happened to modern American political cultivation is that big money has filtered its' way in through big business lobbyist. Unassociated with a vision for the peoples of the countries direction as a whole. Lobbyist, and political party ideology have created a power unseen in the Aim & Purpose of the continued progressive growth of the American political tree. That has produced powerful separatist ideals in political parties, has made oligarchs in politics, in business, and has wedged a large gap in between existing political societies in Washington D.C. This has divided our citizenry with regard for, the Aim & Purpose of creating a new direction for a United States. There is a psychopathic psychology present in the people of our society never before seen. In the evil acts committed by police, and citizens every day. The world sees it when watching media news on TV or while searching the computer internet. Intertwined with a dysfunctional criminal justice judicial system that fails to convict law breakers, a congress which fails to act on gun control. To keep guns away from minors. Or pass into law TSA like searches, metal detector check mandates for every public school and university in America to be safer. At no time in American history has the effects of politicians, police, the medias role, and citizens public behavioral character imposed on the peoples' social life, been so in question! The actions of many people has spawned a sort of separatist segregation in our society. Associated with peoples deep feeling reservations about where they draw the line, on issues that effect their community associations or on public acts which hit close to home. This is a very heavy intake of political food to digest per say, of real issues and feelings that have permeated the airways with a stink after its release. In need of a new political door opening to let fresh oxygen in, water cleansing, and then a touch of scented perfume smell which blots out any lingering existence of the latter American political crisis.

As a university student, public employment professional, or grass root group organizer, you have the ability as I do. To create a sort of coming new work, which can create a re-shaping or reforming of American public systems that the people use. To make them represent the organization you deem appropriate, and at the same time create high functioning systems for public use which are error free. That's if you possess the right aim & purpose. By simply becoming what I call, a player in the game. Being a player in the game is like having a voice in your community, making an educated decision to elect a state or federal representative through a ballet vote in your state. A player doesn't sit the bench, or allow a coach to dictate a players playing time in small increments in critical games. A player in the game is a contributor to the outcome of the game, by making decisive plays to get stops for their team, getting first downs, touchdowns, or getting points for their team to get a win. From a view, the competitors on the battle field are the republicans in the red and the democrats in blue. Who ultimately have a lot of say in dictating how the American legal, and congressional social systems are ran. Didn't cost the competing players to get into the stadium because they created a way for themselves to get in. However, it cost spectators the cost of ticket admission, and as much as they like rooting for their team, they have no control over the outcome of the game. If you analyze real issues which impact American society, and ultimately become widely discussed among people in the public who politic. Many American peoples' lives may in fact be to occupied to feel as if they have time to participate in politics. An a lot of the times they sit the bench, or become spectators, instead of being an active player. As we know, the gaming and sports industry generates billions of dollars every year. Mostly from children, teenagers and adults who enjoy having a controller in their hand to dictate their play achievement in games. If they are playing mind craft, gta, fortnite, nba2k, or madden football. Just as a means of politicking, one could argue the amount of time that children spend in front of the television participating in gaming, is the reason child obesity has increased over the years. Made many children across the country unhealthy couch potatoes, and less physically fit. However, my overall point about gaming is that many people in the public across all ages enjoy, and find time to get involved in the gaming or sport industry. However, that same enthusiasm doesn't transfer within their bosom to become active voices, or players when it involves issues in our society that effect them. When they become of voting age. Spectators or potential players who sit the bench in this game, get taxed on ticket admission at the game in ways they don't like. Moreover, politicians, lobbyists, oligarchs, bankers, and wall streeters are the real players who have been dictating the outcome of the game. As full time participants, utilizing their voice to dictate how our state, federal legislative bodies create public laws. For corporations, banks, and citizens. I have urged constituents in my own community to take a more active role by participating with an active voice. In becoming educated to make better informative decisions to reform parts of our public or governmental social systems. An I urge political science students to take time enough to develop themselves enough to be active participants as players. Who dictate, what may be the very future of American society and the existing systems we have worked to establish. Stay active even if your educational pursuits, and professional employment lead elsewhere outside of the political science realm. Those who aspire to teach in public school classrooms, educate and urge the youth, teens. To grab their controller to be able to dictate public policies, and social systems through their vote as players in the game. By doing this type of work through education in public schools, universities, and law schools. More viable candidates for our criminal justice legal system, states legislatures, and congress could emerge. To turn the unrelenting tide of political issues that has created a plague of black soot on the bottom of the ocean bed, and has left a lasting stain on the waking tide. Fully emerged for the entire American public to see. It is the job of the political scientist to find formidable solutions, and create business networks to re-structure the organization of the many public facets associated with United States political systems.

Duel For Justice

As of late, the American government has experienced some significant changes over the last 12 years. Stemming from peoples' public acts in society which has put pressure on our governmental legislative bodies, and significant party seat changes in Washington D.C's congressional houses. From 8 years of democratic president Barack Obama, and 4 years of republican president Donald Trump. Trump vs. Obama duel, or republican against democrats took its shaping in 2011 and has produced the highest tech weaponry to be used. Similar to the Jefferson vs. Hamilton duel, which posed Anti-federalist against federalist. Although this was not the only person Hamilton would duel against. Nothing like revisiting how the history of the American government began to take its shape. Striking similarities from 1787-1790's definitely relates to public questions being made about the legitimacy of our government in 2018. Questions about the Aim & Purpose of the elected president, and newly elected congress members in a republican majority, and the manner in which legislation is produced. Yet still, two opposing sides having care for how the government is ran, but through very different party affiliation ideologies. As a student of political science, one must ask some serious questions. If the current condition of our American legislative bodies, and people in the public social arena are mentally healthy enough? To render our country's social, political, economic, and functioning governmental systems, a plateau step up from its' condition. In taking a closer look at the existing duel between Republicans vs. Democrats, we could say the government was strong and centralized within the Obama presidential administration. President Obama made use of many executive orders while in office to promote laws which benefited the country. Whereas, Gerry- mandering districts around the country has long been associated with some Republicans who have ran for office. To create a strong centralized Republican congress. However, the concern critique for this party seems to be to attempt to undo what the Obama presidency put in place. Along with undoing Dodd Frank legislation. Republican actions have been similar to Hamilton federalist in that their monetary tax policies, and other legislative changes towards banks along with businesses lean toward the upper class. Differing from federalist, in that the current administration has strongly identified reaffirmation of ties with Israel, who's country is experiencing many turmoils' that have damaged their own identity legitimacy somewhat. The ties with Britain have been strained, and other countries alike who gest with their Trump card like visits to our nation's capital. Mostly, because the current president doesn't come across as being very presidential, and has really made some bad statements in some peoples' views. Which has caused statesmen, country diplomats, and presidents to want to distance themselves from being associated with the American president. This has hurt commerce, in that imposed trade tariffs as a business strategy on China has strained trade and business. Asia has been a large economic market for the United States. While China continues to gain business through large contracts in other parts of the world. American businessmen must have an international business market to sale products to, or to purchase from. Using politics diplomatically gains the trust of other large markets around the globe, which is what the Obama administration attempted to do in Asia and other markets. The Trump administration in their duel with the democrats, has lost track of what strides could have been made. For the fact that China has engaged in trade talks with other countries outside of the U.S. to assist further industrialization, and business development. Where investment has proven to work. The United States could help, with the right political and business gesturing to get a piece of the action. While helping other people. We can agree that it is a proven fact that countries with a strong centralized government, develop industrially, produce a lot of business domestically, and international trade commerce. With countries when willing partnerships, and business contracts can be fortified through the proper diplomatic engagement. That takes into consideration all parties interest.

Time it takes to prepare industrialization food vs.

The time it takes to eat= eat we like

Picture yourself living in a land that had nothing and needing to be cultivated. The aim & purpose of the working people is very driven, and precise perhaps. Due to the fact that their hard work will dictate any means that the people of the society have. Needs for shelter, clothing, food agricultural cultivation, production, and their very means of survival depend upon their evolved branches of knowledge. Which display as proofs of prosperity through the peoples' daily work & systematic organization of meeting their own needs. It's fair to point out that the United States Of America is in a different developmental stage, which is technological. As a dessert of sort, which finalizes the society through a uniquely prepared seven course meal over time. However, the psychology of most human beings that live in different states across America don't represent evolutionary thinking. Unlike earlier working societal contributors. Which contributions of their early work input of knowledge, skill, and labor, assisted the creation of innovative works we now see in the cultivation of the 21st century society. As a farming cultivator, animal care taker, carpenter, clothing weaver, businessman, scientist, technician, engineer, lawyer, or doctor. In the earlier history of our American society, people, and black slaves developed themselves psychologically and through their work to become societal specialist in these vital employment fields. Simply, because people of that era understood the importance of building the land up, having food to make, and creating good organization to sustain themselves in their societal building process. Then later as industrializers through President Franklin D. Roosevelt's signed executive order in 1933. Which created work for people across the country through the works progress administration(WPA). These are the pioneers who created, and prepared the industrialization food which became an American society. Over a long period of generations. Which made it possible for millennials of the 21st century. To constantly eat their fill from intricate parts of societal organization. That is food already created in the form of American society systems, and a plethora of business products. It's easy to argue that some generations of American society have never seen a desolate land, or the work put in to cultivate it into being fruitfully producing from your own sweat labor. My point, is that many people operating in our current society are enjoying the eating of the food. Which is the many existing facets of our industrialized society. Without a care for, the further development of government and systems that pioneers worked voraciously to produce. So it's true, nobody cares about how long it took to cultivate the food, to prepare the food we call industrialized America. However, everybody wants to eat and are eating every day. The congressional duel between republicans and democrats has lead conservatives to pass legislation which deregulates consumer protections to some, by allowing banks and large corporations to function more freely. In republican hands, the consumer financial protection bureau is not serving its' overall governmental purpose. Outside government on wall street, the benefit of insider trading continues to be lucrative for many, and those who break stock trading laws are still not being held accountable through prison confinement. Corporation inversions to other countries continue to hurt jobs for Americans, while the federal government has yet to create larger tax liability for companies who want larger profits with cheaper labor costs. To some people in the public, the larger corporate business industry, and the public congressional social seen full of lobbyists has become an oligarchy. While many Americans sit the bench uninterested in political acts which have a large effect on their public social life. Due to attempting to manage their own interest in personal endeavors, and partaking in enjoying the products that businesses produce. Although we do now see a push from many states public school teachers in Kentucky, and Arizona. An their unions standing up to the states attempting to pass legislation depleting some of their retirement rights. With boistering voices asking the legislators for better salary pay as well. Which in Arizona, educators won a victory when Governor Doug Ducey signed a bill increasing public school teachers' salary in 2018. On a large scale, the problem in the United States remains that many age eligible voters are without many concerns for the further development of the country's government. Its' Laws, public school education, the corporate world, or even public social systems that they may use daily. Being that only a small percentile shows up to the voting polls on election days. It's like people are walking or driving blindly daily with one's head down in their android phone, not wondering what obstacle just may be in their path.

Representative arbitration

We can agree that it was a previous group of people in history, having similar interest in creating a legal doctrine. That would serve as the foundational base for regulating the formation of governing processes as a practical system in America. It is true that the history of our country started modestly, advanced over time into one of the most industrialized lands. That is able to supply its' people with many resources in the form of products for comfortable living. Over the country's many generations, it's obvious that the peoples aim & purpose has differed, the American people have changed, and the peoples' interpretive views of the constitutional doctrine has changed as well. On what is deemed the appropriate method to operate our public social systems, the various branches of our governmental legal system, and the congressional houses. However, there are questions political science students must ask themselves. Is the previous guidance of historians who created our legal constitution relevant to present issues in our American society? Why or why not? What are the relevant issues that have direct impact effects on the peoples' legal social life of our society? Is it mass public shootings, public school shootings, police shooting black people, or being criminalized while being black, dysfunction of our criminal justice judiciary system, and congress as well? Why relevant incidents that impact our communities cause a larger social communication which inevitably create an impact of legal pressure put on state, and federal legislators to rethink their views on legislation? As a political scientist who ask themselves these questions, creates a real focus for having a practical method of guidance. To geographically map out a proposed referendum agenda through arbitration debates of relevant legal issues in law offices, on state, and congressional house floors. Then present formidable legal bills for a vote that detail the litigated text intangibles that are relevant to presenting new laws for the people of America. As a means of grappling with current events that have such a large effect on our society that people create, in various cities, and states around the country. A political scientist who considers all the relevant questions, informational research, and then becomes an arbitrary litigator in this manner creates a better foundational base for success in politics.

The Constitution of the United States

To create formidable solutions for making an arbitrary litigation argument that eventually becomes legal referendum bills in states, or congress in Washington, D.C.. A good student of study must be able to distinguish all the relevant facts in their informational research, and interpret relevant legal information for creating arbitrary litigation on behalf of the people. On current legal issues facing our society, and intertwine that with what the student feels is the purposeful intent of the constitution. Without so much feelings being placed on the relevancy of political party ideology perhaps? My latter statements are introduced because of an inherent feeling that I received after reading the preamble, or as we say the opening of the constitution as a doctrine. The opening specifically makes references to the people of the United States as a whole, and an effort to create the forming of a more perfect union. This written text information in the preamble definitely is a resplendent way of attempting to galvanize the people as a conglomerate for a better United States. We could gather that it's a fair assessment to say that some of the brightest legal minds, revolutionary type thinkers in education, and science at the time, believed in their strengths together. As a means to create organization of a government, other branches as checks and balances, and judiciary legal boundaries for governmental powers to be regulated in order to have a United States. It wouldn't be fair to those studiers of U.S. History, if I didn't mention the fact that there were certain struggles coming from states during the time of attempting to ratify the Constitution. The fact that some states, particularly states that believed in the institution of slavery, had other ideas which prevented these states from joining the union of states in America right away. Struggle resistance persisted through war fights during the civil war of the 1860's, and ultimately the constitution was ratified to form a United States. However, not without the great sacrifice of many black slaves, white people like John Brown, and soldiers who fought in the battles. Another significant question should be asked by the political science student relevant to the time period in history being spoken of here. If the American land was desolate of resources for the people who populated it, without economic industry, and progress towards industrialization what divided them so much which caused such a large war? Which President Abraham Lincoln supported. True that other historian author's like Lerone Bennett Jr. put into real question Lincoln's real objective in supporting the civil war. However, you would think some of the written text wordings in the preamble like justice establishments, insuring domestic tranquility, promote the general welfare, securing the blessings of ones' liberty, and providing for the common defense of what is right for all the people in the land. Would definitely bring people in the states together. However, research on this distinct political period in history details that something greater was at stake for peoples' posterity perhaps? The Constitution ratification kept union troops in the southern states to ensure what seemed to be the abolishment of slavery on plantations, black suffrage, and efforts to ensure the civil rights of people. While any remnants of corporate economic industry, and agricultural production for commerce abroad stood almost at a standstill across the entire country. Social communication among people in the public suggest that there was a large support for the union of the United States Of America. With that, there came a sort of reaffirmation of President Lincoln's administration until his death. Then congress played a major role in creating public reconstruction through their federal legislation. As time progressed over a twelve-year period northerners, and southerners grew tired of fighting one another over the African. The greatly disputed presidential election of 1876 between republican Rutherford B. Hayes vs. Samuel J. Tilden was too close to call. However, congress in 1877 would involve itself in a great compromise with southerners. That would withdraw union troops from southern states. Samuel Gompers would start the American Federation Of Labor, a flood of immigrants would enter into the United States as laborers, while Africans were put back to work on plantations as the backbone making American economic industrialization thrive at home, and abroad through a congressional business scheme.

Article I of the Constitution details the formation of the legislative branch, and that all legislative powers herein granted shall be vested in a congress of the United States, which shall consist of a senate and house of representatives. The house of representatives is stated to be composed of members. Chosen from each state every second year by the people, and the electors in each state shall have the qualifications requisite for electors of the most numerous branch of the state legislature. Our senate of the United States is composed of two senators from each state in the country, chosen by the legislature votes thereof, and each senator or representative in the existing congressional houses get one arbitrary litigation vote. The organization of congress consist of the times, places and manner of holding senator elections, representatives, and shall be prescribed in each state of America by their legislature, but the congress may at any time by law make or alter such regulations. Except as to the places of choosing senator candidates. Powers granted to congress through governmental organization is to lay & collect taxes, to pay U.S. debts, provide for common defenses along with the general welfare of the U.S., all duties and imposts exercises should be uniform throughout the country. Our congress does have powers which are forbidden to it, such as the migration or importation of such persons. As any of the states now existing shall think proper to admit, but shall not be prohibited by the congress prior to the year one thousand eight hundred and eight. A tax or duty may be imposed on such importation, not exceeding ten dollars for each person. States have certain powers which are forbidden to them as well. States cannot enter into treaties, alliance, or confederation, grant letters of marque and reprisal, print coin or bill money, emit bills of credit, make anything but gold and silver coin a tender in payment debts. States cannot pass any bill of attainder, ex post facto law, or law impairing the obligation of contracts, or grant any title of nobility. Article II of the U.S. Constitution attempts to create the organization of the executive branch, which includes the President Of The United States. The executive powers shall be vested in the president. He shall hold his office during the term of a four-year period, and together with the vice president who is chosen for the same term, be elected. However, each state shall appoint, in such a manner as the legislature thereof may direct, a number of electors, equal to the whole number of senators and representatives to which the state may be entitled in the congress. No senator, or representative, or person holding an office of trust or profit under the United States, shall be appointed an elector. Article III the establishment of the judicial branch creates judicial powers for the federal governmental courts, and lays the base foundational framework for states to create judiciary appointments to their courts. The overall judicial power of the United States is vested in one supreme court, and in such inferior courts as the congress may from time to time ordain & establish. The judges, both of the supreme and inferior courts, shall hold their offices during good behavior. An shall, at stated times, receive for their services, a compensation which shall not be diminished during their continuance in holding office. Article IV proves to be a very important part of the Constitution which details the relation of states to each other. The full faith and credit shall be given in each state to the public acts, records, and judicial proceedings of every other state. The congress may by general laws prescribe the manner in which such acts, records, and proceedings shall be proved, and the effect thereof. Moreover, the citizens of each state shall be entitled to all privileges and immunities of citizens in the several states. The federal-state relations are included in this article. New states may be admitted by the congress into this union, but no new state shall be formed or erected within the jurisdiction of any other state, nor any state be formed by the junction of two or more states, or parts of states, without the consent of the legislatures of the states concern as well as of the congress. The congress shall have power to dispose of and make all needful rules and regulations respecting the territory. Or other property belonging to the United States and nothing in this constitution shall be so construed as to prejudice any claims of the United States, or of any particular state. Article V of the Constitution specifically details how to Amend the Constitution as a legal doctrine with two-thirds vote from standing congressional representatives of both houses. Article VI addresses national debts valid against the United States, and recognizes the confederacy. Article VII Ratifying the Constitution, then the Amendments to the Constitution or Bill Of Rights for the people of America. Which some of the Bill Of Rights Amendments began as adopted legal construct through ratification on December 15, 1791. However, students of political science should partake in understanding that true ratification of our constitution did not occur until after the Civil War, and the addition of the 13th, 14th, and 15th constitutional amendments. I will discuss some of the Amendments, but would like to touch some of our discussions on federal-state relations. Being that a lot of public social events, and incidents created by people in our society that express negative sentiment towards others or the country often occur in states. Making local and national media news networks. The publics social outcry commands attention from political lawmakers who suddenly have to make the choice to either elude the voice of the people, to respond through congressional hearings, or create legislation for states legislatures to follow suit. Can you think of all the various incidents which made media news either local or national which involved people from states that got the attention of politicians? Or anything related to political scandal in the Trump, Obama presidential administrations? The judiciary, the justice department, CIA, or FBI? Or in local city governments, and states legislatures? If we are working together and wrote down every such incident or event related to each state along with every city within those states, it would culminate a large list of selected news events. Honestly, from 2012-2019 a lot of covered events by major news media networks involve people, and policing hate crimes in numerous states. These are felonies committed by people that classify as federal hate crimes. Which in analyzing the Constitution about the federal governments state relations, should allow the congress to have more power in creating through the Department Of Justice state investigations. Into the crimes themselves, and the organization along with management of state, or city departments that constitutes any legal protections of the people in states of federal territory. Our federal government in certain situations has announced publicly their investigations into states practices. One overwhelming question that the public, politicians, and federal governmental employees of this democratic republic should be asking about the allocated manpower for investigations in states? Clearly with all the incidents that occur in the states on a daily basis, we can't believe that our federal government has enough employees to conduct a thorough investigation. Into various state, city departments, or persons in the public of questionable acts of character. To support my argument on this particular point, attempt to make note of the number of employees in each of our federal agencies, the numbers don't add up in relation to daily incidents which occur in the American public. Although we do ascertain that when federal investigations do occur that state, and local city governmental officials do work together at times during the investigative process. Moreover, in the Trump presidential administration the FBI Director was fired, the CIA just received a woman appointee in May 2018, The Justice Department has had 3 new appointees to head the agency in the last two years. It's clear that the American public should question the ability of the federal government to adhere to Constitutional legal parameters in federal-state relations. When states miss manage their departmental operational authority during federal crimes committed within their territory. As a politician or head of the executive branch, if you create instability in your administrations ability to carry out daily constitutional authority. Issues from the public trust emerge on members of governments ability to simply establish justice! The prevailing view of what some people would call a democratic republic, is that a prototype organization of government and the management thereof was created on paper long ago. The resounding fact is that both republicans and democrats in America are operating in Washington, D.C. using an experimental political democracy as a means of organizational management. Which is not a preservation of the real legal governmental tradition conferred by the pen on the Constitutional doctrine. As a new land and country of hope, has changed into a more complex cultural enclave to live in. Unlike the country that people like Jocko Graves, George Washington, Alexander Hamilton, Benjamin Franklin, and others during the American Revolution worked to adhere to. Yet, many people still believe and adhere to historical traditions of the American past!

Amendments to the Constitution

The first set of constitutional amendments were initially proposed by the writers, and supporters of the doctrine on September 25, 1789. However, other public events and arbitrary litigation debates among congressmen would prevent the ratification of what would be the first ten amendments to the Constitution. Due to the fact that politicians, and the public from twelve states, felt it was necessary to have specific legal terms sketched out. The first ten amendments are the amended written text created by congress. That would legally protect individuals in the public from unjust acts of government. Better known as the Bill Of Rights. The Bill Of Rights would eventually be conferred through the 1st congressional ratification on December 15, 1791. It is clear that the dichotomy is real, in that many people of the public feared unjust acts from the government. Although there were never any real infractions imposed upon them by governmental officials per say. However, it is much more evident in the 21st century society that people of the public socially complain. About unjust acts of government over taxation, civil rights infringement upon them, reparations for descendants of slaves, corruption bribes for politicians from lobbyists, or misuse of public office for personal monetary gain. By the very people who are either elected or hired as public officials to serve the various city, or state communities around the country. For example, the congressman that served on the House Ways and Means Committee who retired in 2017, other house members convicted of racketeering, tax evasion, fraud, illegally structuring bank transactions in 2017, and the president who plotted with others in Watergate in the 1970's. Moreover, and even a former member of congress who became JFK's presidential election running mate in the 1960's. Being accused of being a part of a presidential assassination plot. In all fairness, this is not to say that all congress members are bad. It's very clear from historical analysis of the 1st congressional appointees, until the current members in 2019, that a trend has developed among American politicians. An the very fear that existed of unjust acts being committed by government on the people in 1791.

That created our Constitutional Amendments or Bill Of Rights. Has manifested a current public fear into American politics that's very real about civil rights infringement, corruption, war proliferation, the inability of the executive branch, and legislative houses to manage governmental affairs for the people effectively. While the history of politics is being re-written through some of my latter statements, and through influential people like Chicago Bulls rebounder Dennis Rodman. Who created the quintessence of trust, which made the meeting between North Korean President Kim Jong Un and American President Donald Trump possible. To establish a diplomatic dialogue, and to be present for the United States query about North Korea as a country. Whose country has been accused of human rights violations against its' own people, and building of rocket nuclear missiles. Meanwhile, America through a supreme diplomacy has had its' eyes on the middle east. Iraq, Afghanistan, Libya, Syria, Iran, Russia, and now talks in Asia. However, it is clear that many in the American public could argue that domestic terrorism is taking place upon many citizens in our own country. And that American leaderships focus has not been fixated on domestic issues. Cleaning up America, the number of gun violence shootings from citizens, gun violence at schools & civil rights infringement on citizens through police. Encouraging reform of criminal justice system, and a current executive branch which fails to keep its' Justice Department along with FBI administration in place. At such a pivotal moment in United States History, it is clear that the current American President has issues with trust. Let's switch gears for a moment to take a closer look at amendments which are currently a large part of congressional, and societal debate among people in the American public. I will only address Amendment 1 Freedom of religion, speech, and the press; rights of assembly and petition. Although many other Constitutional Amendments could be discussed for debate within this reading text.

Since the inception of this amendment, the people of this country have an established means by which to practice freedoms within their own liberty in society. Without feeling like they will be hindered by governmental interference. Now it is very clear that change has impacted our society. America's government and news media outlets have begun to single out Arabs, Mexican immigrants, along with Somalian religious cultures. As secular ethnic menagerie cultures that are in contrast with oligarchs. Who, within their own ideal vision for making America great again, create direct conflicts for people apart of these groups. For example, ICE deportations and what are said to be inhumane momentary jail conditions for immigrants who cross our borders illegally. Like America is still under direct attack. Yet, the majority of attacks on our people are associated through public school shootings done by white kids. Mass shootings in our society are usually associated with white people. To be quite frank, war, mass shootings and tragic killings has been America's epidemic. However, it seems that news media networks in our country for quite some time seemed to centralize a focus of the blame in ethnic communities, on domestic terrorists, or on black on black crimes. Rarely is there ever talk about white on white, Asian on Asian, or Mexican on Mexican crimes. When it's clear that statistical research data proves that people in our country kill where they live. An as gun sales in our country increase, further mass shootings have now become common. People in our society and government have singled out groups to attempt to place blame for current events which effect our entire society. With a polarized stigma being placed on certain groups, with the political intention to construct a mesh of societal resentment. Now large assembly protest on municipal, and state governmental agencies has put a tremendous pressure on politicians in Washington, D.C.. Which from some views of people in the public, has produced an Islamophobia among sects of people who live in America. Unmatched to previous historical decades in the United States. And in some hush hush ways, has attempted to match Islam and Christianity against each other. If there is a Lord God don't both religions serve the same one God? Perhaps this reveals that it's obvious something is wrong with the peoples' rationale in these religions, and not the religions per say? Yet, as of June 19, 2018 the United States Of America has announced a withdrawal from the United Nations Human Rights Council. Citing that current conditions have become appalling, disrespectful for basic rights, and chronic bias against Israel. Really, I don't recall ever hearing any talks about Israel among grass roots groups, various communities I lived in, or in the University Of California Berkeley student lecture halls. It seems more that our government is attempting to decide for us, what countries to align with as allies. However, as a political science student do the research. On the various topics or issues presented in this text and be your own judge of the facts. Then create a written analysis of political thoughts based on what facts you feel you understand. Most importantly, it's a hope that you will discover the trend in our state and federal governmental agencies. The fact that people who peacefully assemble for protest against a lying, or bad government. Or those who don't reflect the American cultural ideals of others in skin tone or through their choice of worship. Are not of us, therefore, neglected on a broader scale. While political ball gestures from politicians that are backed through some media networks. Create rage in some people of the public who commit further acts against those very same people that our government singles out. Which some would debate, that these actions have caused a much larger problem in our very public society. Through the production of more evil acts through people, and government. Keeping certain cultural groups, grass roots organizations, and faith worshippers who are people under attack. With their civil rights illegally being infringed by local governmental agencies, and a federal government who knowingly fails to act on the behalf of the people. Could it be, that we the people in these later generations have simply forgot about Aim & Purpose for mankind alike? While countries are poised to act out aggressions towards one another, and mankind taking weaponry Aim at each other! For those people who claim to be loyal to America, and especially those who hold leadership positions. What are your works if our country and the world is in the condition that its' in? The one thing we should all question. How loyal are other countries who make the claim to be America's allies within our current postings of reviews on the stars & stripes? The actions of many people in our society speaks volumes to the world. In almost a very up close, and personal way now. As the quarterback has taken a knee in the Obama administration, the democratic republic of America has transitioned to a new player in President Trump. Which has caused many influential actors, entertainers, athletes, educational professionals, politicians, and people to respond unlike any other time in American history. As political players willing to do the work to change the scope of our countries direction. As intricate pieces to a team roster which now influence everyday politics in America, but has the world watching as well. Without a doubt people around this world and countries are forming a new review opinion. About the ideals of America as a country, and the power of its' people.

Chapter Two

Foreign Affairs

Enemies of America have been called out. Through strategic provocation of heated conflicts, and through a war of words. As the people of the United States have seen, and listen to the American President refer to the North Korean leader as rocket man during media press conferences. An the North Korean response has been to display their country solidarity with China as a allie. Never the less, democratic leftist or republican rightist through congressional provocation support. As a tendency or natural inclination of their Aim & Purpose. Have kept our military soldiers at war in different countries since 2003. While one American sheriff Joe pushed the fight to attempt to secure the country's borders from illegal migrants. An has now gained further support from the American government. Who has allocated military soldiers to assist border patrol police, ICE, and has pledged a promise to build a border wall in the Southwestern United States. Not without politically charged resistance from Arizona attorney general, the Governor, mayor in Maricopa County, and Mexican immigrants in the community who pushed to vote the sheriff out. Then supported, and still support efforts of bringing an indictment against sheriff Joe, and officers of his staff. For conducting illegal immigration sweeps which targeted the Mexican community in Arizona. The political indictment of Sheriff Joe as being a racist, got him and members of his staff convicted on all charges. However, when President Trump took federal office he gave Sheriff Joe a legal pardon. Meanwhile, there is a new sheriff in town within Maricopa County, Arizona. Illegal migrants coming to America remains a problem to our states, and the federal government. Immigrant dreamers have come from as far as Mexico, Honduras, EL Salvador, Guatemala, Belize, Ecuador, and Brazil over many decades. Many have had legal children born in the U.S., and have worked in this country to build a life. Yet, still hold on to the hope of being able to become naturalized U.S. citizens. As the United States aggressively pursues to protect its borders with immigrant deportations back to their country of origin. American political leadership hasn't expressed much publicly, about reaching out diplomatically to migrant countries to build business industry networks. With the hopes of assisting these countries industrialization development with good intention. Perhaps political, and corporate business diplomats could be a contributing factor to assisting the curtail of migrants wanting to come to America? At any rate, the political ball has been punted away after the offense went three plays and out. The tackle has been made on the punt returner, and it is now time for both teams to exchange the field for offense and defense. Moreover, in other sports areas like the NBA, one of the most talented players have left for the LAKERS. Simply, because the latter team lacked the fire power to be number one in the league every year. As teams on the field transition during games, and players transition to new teams. So does the political ideology of America, and other nations.

Let's transition by switching the gears to burst into orbit, and examine a few other countries who have taken steps to pre-fix their name with new meaning around the world. With the hope of creating a new direction for business recognition, and its' people. All the tribes of South Sudan, Africa have been represented by President Salva Kiir, and President Omar Al-Bashir. Ishmaelite descendants, who derived faith based talks in Khartoum about creating a cease fire on its' people, and talked in depth about the corporate business direction of Africa. Although the President of Ethiopia was not in attendance for this meeting. It is highly speculated among media networks in Africa that he will play a role to circumvent difficulty with corporate business sense. With circumspection respect for opposing sides. Never the less, other political players for the progress of Africa in Ghana, see these regime business talks as a win for the entire recompense of the continent. While internal civil war strife in Syria has decimated its' entire population, and has neutralized the Syrian leader to isolation with countries who oppose his current leadership role. While Russia is supposed to be a strong Syrian allie, not much has been done on the ground to assist a rebuilding process in Syria. Meanwhile, on July 16, 2018 Russian President Vladimir Putin and American President Donald Trump shook hands during a summit meeting in Helsinki. Which some suggest was created from a pageant beauty swooning of Putin, that has corporate business ties intentions of Trump on the back end. Yet, America is in the dark about the Russian president's relationship with a Syrian leader who some oppose. What progress can be made from meeting discussions with the Russians? Will Assad be delivered up to put new leadership in place in Syria? Similar to former Libyan and Iraqi leaders. However, it is very clear that many middle eastern, African, and European countries like Greece who suffered internal corporate business economic collapse. Along with civil wars, have spawned the cause of a widespread refugee and migrant immigrant problem that's out of control. For America, other countries throughout Europe, Jordan, Lebanon, and Turkey. There are at least 68.5 million human beings displaced, 12.6 million are from Syria with

6.3 million being refugees that may have been sent to other countries. However, 6.2 million people are still internally displaced in Syria. The disturbing fact is that half of the total sum of that 68.5 million people who are displaced are children. There are plenty of reports distributed of boats sinking in the Mediterranean Sea, with adults and childrens dead bodies washing up on the banks due to drowning. Just lately in July of 2018, American news media displayed the large uproar from people in our U.S. public on Mexican migrant children being separated from parents at our borders. This political debate caused through media network outlets, and politician reactions forced the U.S. President's hand to create referendum on this issue. Let's be real here, the conditions that Mexican migrants face when they illegally cross the U.S. borders are not as deplorable as the crisis overseas. Yet, there has not been as big a fuss created for millions of innocent children that are displaced, living in dire conditions in camps. There hope has come through UNHCR or the United Nations High Commissioner For Refugees. Foot soldiers of sorts, on the ground who are humanitarians that care about their fellow man. Real people like Amin Awad, Filippo Grandi, Robert Mardini, and many others. Have worked tirelessly with other countries, and religious leaders to make deals to provide some resources for refugees or migrants in camps. Moreover, with such a widespread refugee or migrant immigrant crisis around the world there is never enough resources, or necessary equipment provided in a real effort to help. A massive number of people need assistance, protection, and shelter is urgently needed. Leaders through UNHCR have called on the countries of Japan, Iran, India, Korea, and China to get involved with aiding the United Nations program. Through assisting the rebuilding process of people with prayers, and equipment or providing resources for millions of people who need them. Otherwise, thousands of innocent lives could be lost if urgent action is not taken.

The current American foreign policy through corporate business, and our public educational institutions has been to reach out to international students. Whereas, foreign policy through American politics has tended to have an agenda for creating a social democracy dialogue. As a means of having American interests intertwined with our international relationships with other countries. Through specific policies created to nurture social democratic relations that are deemed appropriate. For countries that America chooses to have relations with. Some would argue that some of America's foreign policy intertwined with providing international students access to higher education institutions, has sparked technological innovation and industrialization production in India. Some are leading corporations in Silicon Valley, other Fortune 500 corporations, and could arguably be leading the student field in electrical engineering at American universities. Meanwhile, the current American foreign affairs policy has tightened, locking the U.S. border doors from access. An the president of America seems to have specialized in having a foreign affairs sovereign agenda, being that the country is at war. However, there now seems to be a switch in the current mainstream attitudes of politicians in Washington D.C.. An attitude that is not so sovereign on foreign affairs now, could be due to the actions of China, North Korea, and uncertainty about the actions of Putin in Russia. If America chooses to take strategic war surge against Assad in Syria. It is definitely true that there are sovereignty wars taking place in other country regions, while America has made a large sovereign surge on countries deemed a part of the Islamic State. The result is that America has been at war for 16 years, a lot of blood has been shed, and now many other countries internationally have their eye on America. Is there a step back in sovereignty wars now that the Trump Administration has dealt with economic issues on China in their own way, met with North Korea, and Russian leaders? Is America using a diplomatic political base as a means for reconciling? While other countries still view America now as a hostile nation that is perpetual in promoting conflict. Meanwhile, America still has a focused foreign affairs agenda in other regions of concern around the globe.

I am sure many American citizens can attest to hearing in media news about Russia supposedly meddling in the last presidential election, and how Russia has vowed to assist Syria if American armed forces get heavily involved in their inner civil war conflict. Many political analysts wonder if politicians, and media are putting the Russian name in the news to sway the American people on viewing Russia's Putin in a certain manner. However, many researchers feel the Russian attention has gained momentum due to their known conflict with Ukraine. And that attempting to tie Russia meddling to American politics, has more to do with putting the country on the hot seat to expose their war conflict with Ukraine. Ukraine is a rural country on a much smaller peninsula that borders Russia. Although some ties to Russia did exist socially, and in a business economic sense. The people of Ukraine don't exactly share the same social and political views as Russians. An has overtime remained an isolated country with its' independence from Russia. Starting near the end of 2013, something changed and Russia a much larger power in the region, began imposing their will on Ukraine's people. Russian military troops and tanks were sent into this much smaller country, sending a shock wave on the almost defenseless people of Ukraine. In the wave of some of the Russian terror imposed on the people of Ukraine, human rights violations, citizen detainment and imprisonment of citizens. Within Ukraine, and some transported back to Russia where some are still being held. In the meantime, Russia has since illegally annexed land in the Crimean Peninsula, Sevastopol, areas near the Black Sea, and near the Sea of Azov. There has also been much violence on the people in Ponetsk, and in Luhansk Ukraine. As a warning to Ukraine from Russia, that says the bigger country won't allow Ukraine to bring Allies to the region. It has been confirmed that some American military troops have made it to the region of Ukraine, to take part in some military training exercises. However, the region geographically is dominated by Russia, which has shifted Ukraine to call on the European Union 28 states. On July 9, 2018 at a summit in Brussels, Belgium. Ukraine's President Petro Poroshenko made strides with the EU to condemn militarization by Russia, annexation, and human rights violations that occurred through violence. Ukraine's governmental leadership has taken the proper strategic steps through the EU to deal wisely with Russia. However, American foreign affairs, and EU officials haven't created an agenda which deteriorates the imposed will of Russia's military on the people of Ukraine. Although America has now met with Russia's president, the problem in curing Ukraine is an all-out war on the Russia front, and in Ukraine. Which foreign affairs analyst, EU member states, and American Armed Forces see war in that region as catastrophic. So as part of a larger foreign affairs agenda in America, Russia remains a topic among American political leaders, media, and the President daily. With the country of Ukraine, and its' peoples struggles in mind.

Moving swiftly to another geographic region in the world. Which American politicians, the President, religious scholars, and many people of our public take interest in, is Israel. For a long time, American foreign policy has been to strategically aid Israel in creating a social democracy through appointing leadership through voting elections. To strengthen its' quest in maintaining their current border regions with military troop training, and stock piling the necessary weaponry equipment. Paid for by Israel, and supplied by American allies. It would be an understatement to say that Israel has had a large influence on American politics, our economic system, the formation of some American banks, and the Federal Reserve Bank in Washington D.C.. Since the inception of the Federal Reserve Bank Almost every chairman has been a Jewish person, and Israel has influenced American politics with Jewish congressmen. From a foreign affairs perspective Israel does remain an American partner, very evident through both countries leadership relationships. However, as Israel has transitioned its' country as a stronghold in its' region. The country has failed its' moral responsibility in recognizing its' Palestinian borders, and has made borders of the entire country more volatile. Through a long standing conflict with Islam. Over time Israel has lossed the moral ground stance, that the country once liked to be recognized upon. Very evident through political spats between Israeli leadership, and the White House. On the Palestinian state, refugees in Israel being put on notice to leave the country within 90 days, and some Jews who live in Israel not being able to have their families visit them from other countries. American foreign policy has candidly addressed some of these major issues with Israeli leadership. However, it is clear the region of Israel has become more volatile by the day, as reports come in about many human rights infringements on Israeli citizens by Jewish soldiers, racism towards its' ethnic Jewish population, and Palestinian attacks on Israeli citizens. As American foreign policy towards Israel remains hopeful, it is a definite that Israel remains uncapable to be candor in its' ability to rectify clear problems facing its' country. While the country fails in many respects to partake in any other humanitarian efforts around the globe. As many around the world now fail to see the recondite base of our Lord that Israel has attempted to stand upon in their country's own foreign policy. An as what many Americans see as their sort of moral base for courting American allie ship. Politicians in America can't deny that Israel's region is in chaos! As many concerned people of faith now have their eyes on the country of Israel. While leading the charge for change in Israeli politics, and society from country regions elsewhere.

For a long time, Europe has never really experienced very many real issues which has had serious effects on its' people, and society. However, it seems that internal tention about the socio-economic lifestyle of many who are part of ethnic groups in the United Kingdom. Slowly began to make people who were non-native, or refugee migrants feel as if their working lives among native Europeans is at risk. At risk to only achieving bear minimum living conditions on substandard employment salaries, without broader access in European corporate business to create jobs, and employment that says broader visions of good life exist for many. Arguably, Europe has always been a gateway for people who want to study at a University abroad. Whereas, many other countries top schools have not been accessible for other countries students who want to study abroad. Even American colleges, have only been open and accessible to droves of international students in our more recent history. However, the invention of the computer internet has connected many people, and students of education around the world globe. The fact remains that hostilities among natives who feel infiltrated to other nations peoples' problems being brought to their borders. While some non-native Europeans, or refugee migrants feel their life is confined to home living standards that are more like condensed burrows. Studiers of worldly events which have impacted an effect on the European people and their society as well, has been America's war proliferation on Islamic terrorists. What sparked problems in Europe as well was the very demeaning portrayal of Muhammad-Ibn-Abdullah the messenger of Allah, through what was thought to be funny cartoon characters. Which many people of faith in various religious sects, took as a degrading attack on the Lord. The reaction created a karma like intuition in multiple countries, that has sense spawned an intertwined societal activism through very brutal terrorist attacks on European society. Attacks have been data based reported in

Finland, Germany, Sweden, Spain, France, on the London Bridge, at the Manchester Arena, and infringed attacks on pedestrians with vehicles. Now government, Law enforcement officials, and security are on high alert in these countries. Moreover, it is a daily task for Law enforcement officials to attempt to protect the people in society, and through investigative attempts identify suspected terrorists who plan harmful attacks. Arguably, it is the actions of many people or countries on both sides of these complex issues that has made European society in 2018 a hot bed for instability. Furthermore, the slowing of corporate business economic growth on a larger scale among European Union nations made them unable to repay or refinance their governments accrued debts as a bailout. Creating over indebted banks in Greece, Spain, Portugal, Ireland, and Cyprus. Causing some banks to shut down completely, while holding on to citizens' Euro currency sitting in bank accounts. This caused societal instability as some citizens rioted in the streets, and denounced trust of the government along with elected officials. Ultimately, these countries did seek help from other countries in the form of monetary loans through the European Central Bank. Which the United Kingdom played a role within these countries financial banking crisis. However, American foreign policy towards Europe prompted congressional hearings to be held in our nation's capital Washington, D.C.. On the future sustainability of certain European nations, and the specific causation criteria that created the financial crisis of certain European Union nations as well. Somehow the American government flooded the Eurozone with monetary loans through the International Monetary Fund. In an effort to assist European governmental debt, corporate business, and the financial banking crisis in the Eurozone. Although large numbers of unemployed people in many European countries still existed as of 2013. The United Kingdom's abrupt decision to exit the use of the Euro is re-shaping the Eurozone. Meaning that the United Kingdom is withdrawing as a Eurozone member-state voluntarily, and will supposedly cease using the Euro as a national currency. This official severance or Brexit, is slated for March 29, 2019. In 2018 there is a persistent rise in the number of immigrant migrants, and refugees from war torn countries looking for asylum. In some of the already troubled countries of European Union member-states. One can wonder about uncertainty, but truth says that governments, and parliamentary leadership, along with citizens must be at the forefront of innovative change to the structure of society. In relation to the structure of legal referendum or parliament laws that they create. And with a fair effort that pushes towards the betterment of peoples lives in an industrialized socio-economic corporate business world. Where hard work brings about the never ending production of fruits, more than adequate monetary compensation from employment, and the necessary equipment to build castle homes of prosperity.

Many researchers on American foreign affairs would arguably exclaim that America has only attempted a minimal pitch for progress towards social democracy in the middle east. Or predominately countries with real people that live within an Islamic religion perfected for them as Muslims. Currently in 2018, many people debate about there being an opposite shift in foreign affairs policy towards all Islamic nations. It's fair to say that it is because of the attacks on the twin towers in the state of New York. By two terrorists who hijacked two domestic airline planes in America on 9/11, is the cause for America's war on Islam. Or war against the Islamic State. Some researchers would classify fighters in Iraq as the Islamic State. However, for classification in this text we will group those who fight for Islam as the Islamic State, Isil, Islamic terrorists, Taliban, Al-Qaeda, and Boko Haram. Other people who were said to be organizers of militant Islamic groups in their respective countries, or within the regions of Islamic countries were Osama Bin

Laden, Saddam Hussein, and Muammar Gaddafi. While American foreign affairs policy towards the middle east has sparked proliferated war in multiple countries, it is true that American military armed forces have eliminated bad factions of Islamic fighters who created terror on their own people within their respective countries. For example, in countries like Iraq where Hussein supporters tortured some citizens who differed with the ruler on leadership ideology, and in Afghanistan where the Taliban has threatened citizens in rural areas. About giving information or supporting American military soldiers in the region. Doing such things could constitute a death sentence for citizens who live under such war conditions within these countries. The overwhelming fact which seems to be unreported about American foreign policy towards war in these countries, is the large number of deaths of innocent women and children. From intense ground war battles between the two factions, and the use of drones to drop bombs on suspected Islamic State strongholds. This U.S. policy for some, fits the nature of its purposeful calling, while it seems that a fear of hell has become the reality of country devastation in middle eastern countries. As millions are displaced within their own country, refugee, migrant immigrant number percentages increase for Europe. While America as a country in attempting to deal with its' foreign affairs policy internationally, has become an internal civil mess all at the same time. Some researchers who study industrialized civil societies would argue that the result of countries facing so many real public issues regarding citizens unrest with governmental policies, is simply karma. In turn, this has seemed to awaken a new wave of terror activists across the globe, some who are not a part of the Islamic State. However, all these terrorists feel their objective is to voice their dissatisfaction with countries or society by hurting other people. To render solutions to societal problems congressional leadership, educators, clinicians, and students must ask the question of who's at fault for creating such influential psychology in the people of their societies? Then form a base for an American foreign policy that is suitable for combating foreign enemies, and has an overwhelming support of many people within our society. It seems that all these countries have lawmakers, executors of the laws that oversee citizens, and citizens breaking laws. By creating civil unrest for their whole society through murder of other people. Which expresses that the Aim & Purpose of their overall governmental policies have failed, and is not an inherent of nature that gives an internalized good feeling to their respective citizenry in their countries. Never the less percentage numbers exclaim that extreme acts of terrorism on citizens in America, and around the European world are on the rise.

Iran in the 1970's was a country looking for a new identity, and although the people of America didn't know much about the people of Iran. Our United States government during this time period, did possess a foreign affairs policy objective in Iran. Which ultimately caused civil unrest that overthrew the Shah of Iran, and really set the historical stage for the evolution of the new Iranian governmental leadership along with the people of Iran to rebuild their country with Aim & Purpose. Which produced the establishment of work towards having a legitimate country with corporate business industry around some of its' oil reserves. To be recognized as a legitimate economic power. In order for Iran to create such stability for themselves, top universities propagated the re-education of their citizenry, utilizing parts of American democracy in their choosing of governmental leadership through an electoral voting process, and began adopting some ways of other countries modern culture. Which is now recognized around the world through not just their oil industry, but through other products that are made for export in Iran, and even fashion trends. This is the Iran we know in 2018, but American foreign policy towards presidential leaders whom our government felt didn't represent our business interest. At times painted a different picture of good men, and depicted the country in a more negative light. While American foreign affairs objective has long been to attempt to control Iran's economic production of oil exports with the rest of the world. By constantly attempting to control the economic success of Iran, by bargaining American Allie ties with Europe and other countries where U.S. influence exist to stifle real corporate business contracts. While painting a corrupt picture of the Iranian leadership, and questioning the country's military prowess on attempting to develop nuclear bomb capabilities. For example, such a leader in Iran is Mahmoud Ahmadinejad who suffered under America's strategic foreign affairs tactics on Iran. This Iranian leader visited the United States, and specifically addressed Iran as a country. Through a speech at the United Nations headquarters in New York. However, America's foreign policy towards other Muslim nations such as the country of Saudi Arabia, has been more of an equal partnership in working together. Working together on America's strategic interest in other predominately Muslim nations, and on issues regarding American strategic military readiness within the Saudi geographic region. Due to the current American foreign affairs policy towards Iran as a country, corporate business contracts on a large scale for imports of Iranian products to the U.S. have been minimal or almost void. However, Iran has made business partners with other nations for imports and exports of certain products. Ranging from oil, clothing fashion, spices, rugs, and machinery. While Iran's new generation of people are pushing a positive view of its' country to other foreign countries, and are engaging in some international student exchanges at top universities around the world. While the government of Iran works on permitting its' Muslim citizenry to have more free access to connect to the world through computer technology internet.

American armed forces are among some of the greatest strategic battle fighting troops on the planet. War itself, is always of great cost to the countries who start them, the real people who fight wars, and the congressional legislators who find it necessary to declare war against a particular enemy. Due to the fact that bloodshed enters into countries conflicts with one another, and there is a large accountability to the many families who lose loved ones that fight in war conflicts. However, American foreign policy litigators have been at war in various middle eastern or Muslim countries for 16 years and counting. Many armed forces war strategist, and research studiers on American war conflicts would agree that most war conflicts usually end with a victor. In analysis of American foreign affairs policy on the war in Afghanistan, my latter statement about a victor within the conflict is not the case for the United States. America has been spreading itself thin for many years now with thousands of armed forces troops in various Muslim countries. Pushing the foreign policy objective at first, on finding Osama Bin Laden. Then using the attention on Bin Laden in American Media sectors to gain the American peoples support for a war in Afghanistan. As if a small militant Islamic group called the Taliban in this country, was harboring Bin Laden from U.S. capture. Which was far from the truth. The result, is that are American armed forces began a war in Afghanistan on the Taliban. Now there are American troops in the region, other countries which border the Afghani region have now sent other troop support to aid the Taliban. An now the war in Afghanistan has lingered on for 16 years. With American and Nato lead troop reinforcements fighting an enemy they don't know now. Due to the fact that some Taliban forces may in fact be fighting American troops for occupation of their country, but Islamic State troops from other regions are fighting sternly against Americans. An the citizens of Afghanistan are now being threatened, and killed by American troops, and Islamic State fighters for cooperating to give any information to Americans on their strategic headquarters. Most recently in 2018 suicide bombings in Kandahar, and in Kabul have killed at least 50 people. Which states there is a failure to create a stabilization in Afghanistan with American troop occupation. There are reports of American troops forcefully making Muslim women remove their hijabs, and having sex with Muslim women in these countries. With troop occupation not making a difference in Afghanistan, it has caused a rise in the number of innocent civilian casualties. It seems that the war cannot be halted or stopped, that maybe the war can't be won, and that American foreign affairs policy objective forbids the troops from leaving the Afghan region completely. It seems that some of the truth in this war conflict that has been proliferated from both sides in the battle, is that on the ground wars can't be avoided by America. Long ago America began the strategic attempt to change some of its' war strategy with the introduction of the drone, satellites', and the pursuit of strategic missile defenses. Which has cost our country in the hundreds of billions of dollars since the Reagan presidential Administration. Moreover, the Afghan President Ashraf Ghani did present a plan for cease fire in February 2018, and current American President Donald Trump has countered by unveiling a fight to win policy in the Afghani region. Now 3,000 additional troops have been sent to Afghanistan for initiating armed forces tactical operations in countering extreme terrorism. In addition, other Nato allies are being asked by America to do more to help in the country region.

A good political science student should analyze with a good glance, America's current foreign affairs policy. With extensive research, talks with other political scientists in the field, and societal surveys on citizens. To really get a good feel on Americans feelings about the current foreign affairs policy. In closing, there is an attempt to provide a brief history of some of America's centralized focus in certain countries within this chapter of the book. However, the United States of America's government does conduct some type of diplomatic relationship with over 200 nations internationally around the planet. With a dignified demeanor that had been long standing to promote a diplomatic social democracy, industrialization, and corporate business industry. With a respect for other sovereign countries as a nation, and that these countries possess the highest authority over its' own border region territories. Many political science research analysts now argue that there has been a complete shift in America's Foreign Affairs Policy objective on my latter statement. Many other countries now have their eyes fixated on the U.S.. Simply, because America has proliferated war on a large scale in many country regions that includes occupation of their territory. Which other nations that watch America's actions feel that our country is playing the big sovereign role with not only war, but with economic sanctions which threatens other countries socio-economic lifestyle perhaps. Most importantly, feeling a little uneasy in that America no longer respects other nations states sovereignty as equal. An feel that American political leadership with the use of a show of its' U.S. armed forces power, has a Aim & Purpose of wanting to attempt to bully other nations. While fear of having their countries border regions infiltrated and occupied has many large countries military at heightened security readiness alerts. It could be viewed that America's current foreign affairs policy is one that promotes a fight conflict, and makes the international world a more volatile place towards Americans. Not the type of foreign affairs policy objectives our country should continue to have, in a technological age that is finally connecting us to people around the world. More hot pockets around the world with potential war conflicts that are volatile with large countries is not what our diplomacy should promote. If we as a country want to indicate through our actions, a sustainable dominion over the earth. As the fruit of many generations of people continue to come forth, and many business type innovations that make the lives of many people around the world better continue to be produced. We the people, as political scientists or governmental leadership officials, must always remember that we have a choice in attempting to create new directions for America or other countries. Through creation of suitable foreign affairs policy objectives. That express a complete method for the operation of government, the socio-economic direction of any given countries citizens through the creation of proper industrialization projects, and corporate business structure for job creation.

Chapter Three

Operating Governmental Affairs

The United States Government is comprised with intricate departmental pieces as a means for our President, and his appointed employee cabinet members to run the complete operations of the American government. Protecting the people of America through a fully operational governing system only occurs after an elected president takes the initiative to quickly appoint selected cabinet members. So that congress can approve these employee cabinet members through congressional hearings. Then these newly appointed governmental officials can then begin the process of joining the department that they have been appointed to serve. To ensure that these federal departmental agencies are being ran with the highest employee competency level. As a benefit to the citizens of America, and the country by providing complete systematic services. Through the work operations of appointed employees to the presidential cabinet departmental agencies. This is the building of a base foundational framework for the prototype governing system that is operating. Good political science students must still ask questions though. Are all the cabinet departments of our federal government's functioning operations systematically intact through the work support of our elected president? However, the fact still remains is that the President of the United States is the acting head of state, head of the American government, while serving as the armed forces commander-in-chief. Which includes the responsibility of keeping updates on new congressional referendum in order to implement and enforce governmental laws written by the congress. Along with utilizing adequate business resources to create appointments who head federal government agencies, which includes the cabinet. Our president deals with about 50 independent federal commissions appointees as well. There are approximately fifteen executive departments, and Article II of the United States Constitution dispenses power of responsibility to our president. For any execution and the enforcement of federal governmental laws created by congress. Through the president's leading appointee members' heads of the cabinet. Let's examine some of the existing cabinet departments that proceed to carry out the day to day administrative operations of federal governmental cabinet agencies.

The Department OF Defense is located in Arlington, Virginia. Lead by experienced four star generals within the American armed forces ranks. The armed forces departments are made up of the Marines, Army, Navy, Air Force, the joint chiefs of staff, National Security Agency, Pentagon Force Protection Agency, and the Defense Intelligence Agency. There are other agencies at the Pentagon, offices, and military command centers as well. All meet with the American president to be briefed on diplomatic relations with other countries, and to report pertinent information as directed to the president. On issues related to national security, needed equipment, soldiers' moral, or on strategic operations within military war conflicts. Most importantly, the Department OF Defense main mission is to provide adequate military force protections through their agency. To attempt to protect the security of the country, and to withstand or avoid war with a show of force. The Department is diverse in that it has men and women who serve. Roughly a combined 1.5 million people serve on active duty status, 1.2 million citizens serve as reserve forces in the National Guard, and there are nearly 701,000 civilian personnel working for the department in some capacity. A broad range agency where the personnel applicable abilities protect America's national interests. Through strategic war fighting, providing humanitarian assistance to countries in need of disaster relief, and performing military peacekeeping operations. This department also has the very difficult task of organizing the strategic protection of the American president. During any of his or her travels outside of the country internationally. This department is a vital help in assisting American citizens' daily life, ensuring security support. With a moral of alacrity coming from American soldier troops, who are armed with strategic equipment, and thinking mechanisms which serve as purposeful protections of the people of America. This departmental agency is unmatched in its' allegiance or strong support obligations that it has to American citizens, and to the operations of government services.

The Department OF Agriculture is a vital agency that arguably provides its' services to every person in America in some way shape or form. The United States Secretary Of Agriculture administers all of the operations, and management of the USDA through 100,000 employed workers. This department is vast in its' outreach to American citizens in that it attempts to regulate Americans getting healthy products. By partnering with the Food and Drug Administration in grocery stores around the country. Working with grocery stores to create legal regulations for how products are stored, packaged, sold to American citizens, and on the removal of expired products from store shelves. The U.S. Department Of Agriculture's complete development and execution of management operations policies within our country are on providing ways for producing healthy food, agriculture, and farming. While the departmental aim in operational management execution includes working with farmers, meat producing ranchers, while placing focus on promoting agricultural production. This federal governmental agency advances innovative ideas on assuring food safety, promoting agricultural trade through commerce, protecting natural resources, fostering rural community areas, and ending hunger starvation around the globe. USDA aid programs through the United Nations play an important role overseas at times, by providing surplus foods to people displaced in war torn countries, refugees who live in camps, and developing countries as well. The USDA has an annual operational budget of approximately $96 billion. The departmental operations management includes 17 internal agencies. For example, the Food and Nutrition Service, the Animal and Plant Health Inspection Service, and the Forest Service as well. A large allocation of the departmental budget is given to mandatory programs which are required by federal laws. These particular programs are designed to provide types of nutrition assistance, promote agricultural exports from America, and to attempt to work with scientists to conserve our environment.

The Secretary Of Commerce conducts the day to day management and agency operations of the federal governments Department OF Commerce. With approximately 38,050 internal employees who work for the department in various task forms, and an annual budget allocation of $6.6 billion in resource funds towards departmental operations. The Department OF Commerce conducts the federal governments business in multiple ways. Which aids our American citizenry, and the corporate business industry structure. That produces an assortment of products Americans use daily. This governmental agency is very known for playing a very vital role in the American governments trade policies with other countries. By creating new trade agreements to assist American exports, and imports of business products from international countries. Employees who work for the Department OF Commerce do this type of work to create agreements. By helping to promote U.S. exports which derive from American corporations who produce good products. Moreover, the people who work for this agency assist the legal enforcement of international trade agreements that are created by U.S. corporations with other countries businesses internationally. Which includes regulating all legal parts of business trade contracts, the overseeing of the storage of products, and for the regulation of product shipments to U.S. borders as well. Through creative efforts to run the Commerce Department in this manner, the federal governmental agency has tasked itself with improving American citizens living standards, and promoting American economic development. This is how the Departmental agency creates support for U.S. businesses. By gathering economic data, certain demographic data information, while industrial industry is created for developing countries through many services. The Department OF Commerce as a federal agency which serves the American people. Also engages in other services as formulating technology, telecommunications policy, and ensuring the use of effective technical resources. This includes improving scientific understanding of our environment, oceanic life, and ensuring the proper use of researched scientific information. The federal agency also issues patents, and trademarks as well.

The Department OF Education is a federal governmental agency, within the cabinet of the American president's executive branch. This agency creates specific educational strategies which attempt to promote a higher learning level of public school students' achievement in states. The objective of the Department OF Education is to create incentive goals for higher learning levels in students' state school testing scores. The school districts within our country whose students display higher achieving level test scores. That meet federal Department OF Education guidelines, their school districts receive extra monetary funding from our federal government. Such recent departmental program for promoting a higher level of schools' students' achievement, and preparation for competition in an international economy was race to the top. A program during the Obama presidential administration. A way in which students have continually utilized competition to bring out the best in their achievement. For American students to be able to compete in a global economy with other students on an international scale. This includes private schools, charter schools, and home schools throughout America. With regard for, incentive guides which improve students' education quality, attempting to foster students' educational excellence, and with hope to ensure the reduction of segregation to safeguard a real equal access to educational opportunity. Other vital services which play a role in strategic efforts to assist American & international students, is collecting data on U.S. schools to guide improvements in the quality of education provided to students through teachers, and school districts. This includes working closely with state, local governments, parents, and school students. Another service which some feel is a major resource for students through the Education Department is the administering of federal financial aid for college education. In all this cabinet agency has 4,201 employees working in the day to day operations under the U.S. Secretary OF Education's managerial oversight. The budget allocation for the running of the department is roughly $68.6 billion annually.

The Department OF Energy is an agency which has become more innovative as of late. In its' mission to work closely with inventors, and scientists to advance finding new energy sources which are cleaner. In addition to its' mission of creating advancement of the national, economic, and security of the United States. The Department OF Energy works closely with scientific researchers on energy through electric companies, home builders, and even agriculture farmers to promote American energy security for the future. Even business corporations conduct work with the DOE. All in an effort to encourage many developments of clean, reliable, and affordable energy sources. Federal funding from the DOE budget is often administered to encourage scientific research. Which furthers the purposeful goal of discovery, and innovation in energy sources. Each time a new energy product is created, and becomes marketable this ensures American economic competitiveness. While creating a base foundation stronghold for improving the quality of life for American citizens, and the international world. Over 100,000 federal, and contract employees assist in the departmental work to make future developments a reality. However, the United States Secretary OF Energy is also tasked with overseeing and ensuring our country's nuclear security. An creating strategic plans for environmental protections that provide adequate resolutions to the legacy of proliferation in nuclear weapons production. The Secretary OF Energy has an annual budget of $23 billion to assist work efforts in overseeing this executive branch cabinet agency.

The Department OF Health And Human Services is a federal governmental agency. Who's working mission directive, is principled around protecting the health of all American citizens. Through providing human services that are adequately essential to the best health of our citizens. Most importantly, these services are catered especially for those U.S. citizens who are least able to help themselves. There are various existing agencies within the health and human services department. There are 11 operating divisions which include 8 agencies in the public health service, and 3 human services agencies. These working agencies focus on different areas within health and human services. Such as gathering data through conducting social science research on citizens, or on health through medical discovery publications. This agency works closely with states to create strategic Medicaid, Medicare health programs to provide to one in four American citizens health insurance. An works to prevent disease outbreaks. This department works with the Food and Drug Administration closely to assure food and drug safety as well. This departmental agency does work closely with medical physicians, the surgeon general, and does value the opinions of the surgeon general as well. The Secretary OF Health and Human Services has working oversight in the Food and Drug Administration, the Centers for Disease Control, and the National Institutes of Health. While 65,000 working employees assist this departmental agency in its' efforts to reach goal objectives. With an existing annual budget of $700 billion.

The Department OF Homeland Security is a vital cabinet agency. The Homeland Security Act of 2002 established this department. Mostly, in response to the attacks by terrorists on the twin towers in New York on September 11, 2001. This department directs its' focus on securing or protecting the American continent. This type of attention focus through this particular departmental agency protects the lives of the American people. Through the attempt to disrupt or prevent terrorist type attacks on our people within the states. Moreover, protecting the critical geographic infrastructure of our nation, and its' key resource preserves. While possessing officer man power, who have the knowledge, the skill ability to respond to incidents that do occur around this nation. Through criminal investigations of possible perpetrators of terrorist type crimes to divert incidents within our borders. An equipped officers who directly confront terrorists in combat. There are many facets to the Department OF Homeland Security which now consolidates 22 executive branch agencies. This includes U.S. Customs Services, U.S. Secret Service, the U.S. Coast Guard, Transportation Security

Administration, and the Federal Emergency Management Agency. This is the U.S. president's third largest cabinet department which employs roughly 216,000 people. In its' mission to assist border patrol in securing American borders, to protect travelers through its' TSA association, our transportation infrastructure, legal enforcement of immigration, while responding to emergency disasters. This agency also offers certain trainings to American citizens on preparedness, and emergency prevention. A new policy coordinated by the Council of Homeland Security at the White House in Washington, D.C.. In a collaboration with other defense, federal & municipal intelligence agencies, which are led by the Assistant to the President for Homeland Security.

The Department OF Housing And Urban Development, is ran by The Secretary Of Housing and Urban Development Dr. Ben Carson. Better known as HUD, is a federal agency within the presidential cabinet. Mainly responsible for addressing the housing needs of Americans. Most national policies, and programs around the housing needs of many Americans are created within this department. Mostly, with a focus to develop strategic HUD programs, and affordable housing plans geographically within states. As an aim to improve many of our nations communities, and to enforce created fair housing laws around America. For many people in our country, the idea of homeownership or renting is ideal for creating a base foundation to building a family and humble abode. An HUD makes major monetary contributions to supporting peoples dream quest of homeownership. The Department OF Housing And Urban Development support through programs that are for lower and moderate income families. These business programs assist with homeownership financing or renting through its mortgage insurance, and a type of rent subsidy program. There are other departmental agencies within the larger HUD base, such as the Federal Housing Administration. The Federal Housing Administration provides the resource of mortgages, and loan insurance to people. Another agency within the department is the Office of Fair Housing and Equal Opportunity, which assist with ensuring all Americans an equal access to the housing of their choice in any state community. Our country has had problems with housing discrimination in the past, and this agency attempts to guarantee people access while ensuring fair play in business practices on our citizens. Another inner agency asset is the Community Development Block Grant Program. Which offers citizens job employment opportunities, assist with helping many city communities develop economically through practical business ideas, and provides certain city areas with housing rehabilitation. Public housing and homeless assistance programs are facilitated administratively through HUD as well. There are about 9,000 employees who oversee the day to day operations of the entire departmental agency. The annual budget for the Department OF Housing AND Urban Development is roughly $40 billion.

The Department OF The Interior is an agency concerned about conservation in our country. The overall mission in its' operations and management is to primarily create strategic work focus on protecting American natural resources. Other featured operations within this departmental work load are conducting scientific research to better understand the how to, in conserving precious natural resources. As well as conserve and protect fish and game wildlife. This agency also Offers recreation opportunities through national parks, while tasked with protecting the endangered species in the parks. DOI creates fact based focus to honor American Indian tribes through the bureau of Indian affairs. This includes Alaskan Natives, and some responsibilities to island communities also. Moreover, the Department OF The Interior manages hundreds of dams, reservoirs, and 500 million acres of surface land which is equivalent to one-fifth of the land in America. Other agencies that exist within the Department OF The Interior are the U.S. Geological Survey, and the Minerals Management Service. The DOI is one of a few cabinet agencies that raises billions of monetary dollars outside its' allocated budget every year. Through timber leases, recreational permits, land sales, minerals, energy, and grazing. The Secretary of the Interior runs the management of this agency , while 70,000 employees and 200,000 volunteers manage the day to day departmental work operations. The annual budget allocation for this agency is $16 billion 500 million.

The management of the Department OF Justice is overseen by the Attorney General. Who is the chief Law enforcement officer of the American Federal government. Which as of late, has experienced great turmoil under two different presidential administrations. Partly due to the fact that there have been three different Attorney Generals in about three years. Under our last two American Presidents. With that stated, it is the Attorney General's working job through the Department OF Justice to provide expert leadership for our federal justice system. To enforce the Laws, to prevent, and control crimes regardless if the criminal threats are foreign or domestic. An through the appropriate justice court designated, seeking to justly punish law offenders who are guilty of unlawful behaviors. Through a court proceedings process that ensures fairness, and impartial administering of justice for all Americans. Moreover, the Attorney General does represent the United States in court legal matters. While giving legal business advisement to the President Of The United States, and other heads of the executive departments of our American federal government. The Attorney General does appear before congress in arbitrary hearings, and occasionally appears in person before the Supreme Court justices. There are approximately 40 component organizations which make up the Department OF Justice. This includes the Federal Bureau Of Investigations, Drug

Enforcement Administration, U.S. Marshals, and the Federal Bureau Of Prisons. Due to the DOJ being a Law enforcement agency, the number of employees within the department is classified information. However, the annual budget for this agency is around $25 billion, as the central agency to enforce our federal laws. Lastly, on record the DOJ is the largest law office in the world.

The Department OF Labor is an agency which oversees, and administers federal program apprenticeships in a variety of work trades. These federal programs are designed for American citizens to address new job trainings, and keeping employment work conditions safe. The Labor Department also regulates the minimum hourly wage people are paid on a job, overtime pay, unemployment insurance, and problematic employment discrimination issues. In a legal partnership created with the Equal Employment Opportunity Commission. The focused operations of this agency attempts to create, and ensure a stronger American workforce. Through strategic missions which foster, and promote the work training development of American job seekers. For their personal welfare as on the job wage earners, and improved working conditions on the job that produce over the long term more retirees in United States corporations. While creating a new plateau for a socio- economic rise in the American standard of living. This agency also works closely with corporations to create viable opportunities for profitable employment. By helping employers find good workers. An is involved in creating training trends for technology, while offering many other services. Like advancing peoples work training skills, protecting their retirement & health care benefits, and Strengthening free collective bargaining. Other service programs are created through the tracking of changes in employment skill trends. Offices within the Department OF Labor who offer services include the Bureau Of Labor Statistics. Which tracks the data number of employed citizens in America through corporations, and those people who are unemployed as well. This math data number information is then comprised, made into readable graphs, then offered for public review, and to economists. All as a means of having national economic measurements of departmental work operations. Another office that works within this agency are the Occupational Safety&Health Administration. Responsible for promoting the safety, and health of American citizens who are working men and women. The federal government's principal statistics agency for labor economics is included in the Department OF Labor as well. While the Secretary OF Labor oversees& manages these departmental agencies, there are approximately 15,000 employees involved in the day to day work operations of the entire Labor Department. The annual budget allocation for this cabinet department is $50 billion.

The Department OF State is a cabinet agency ran by the Secretary Of State. Under most circumstances the Secretary plays a vital role in attempting to aid the United States President. By taking a leading role in strategically developing, and carrying out some of the implementation of agenda focused areas in America's foreign policy objectives. As the U.S. President's top foreign policy advisor. The Secretary Of state maintains firm responsibilities which include adequate representation of the United States ideology internationally. Current efforts of diplomacy through the State Department, is maintaining diplomatic relations with approximately 180 countries around the world globe. Other critical services offered through the Secretary's responsibilities. Are giving other countries foreign assistance, creating foreign military training programs, countering international crime rings, and partnering with the United Nations through UNHCR to assist refugees. As well as offering a plethora of services to Mexicans, foreign nationals, and U.S. citizens seeking entrance into America. The Department OF State has U.S. foreign service employees, which includes international organizations in some countries abroad. There are 5,000 American civilian workers within the agency, and approximately 30,000 employees who work in the department carrying out the day to day mission operations for the Secretary Of State. The annual budget allocation for this cabinet agency is approximately $35 billion.

The Department OF Transportation has a mission focus of creating transportation systems which are convenient, and accessible to the entire American public. While ensuring that the system of transportation is safe, fast, and efficient in its' use purpose. Moreover, this departmental agency is innovative in utilizing the best technology to create photographic maps of perspective geographic areas in the United States. That are viable areas to create new transportation systems, and in city communities where transport exist but needs improvement. Utilizing departmental work operations through approximately 55,000 employees makes the convenience of transportation systems for American citizens possible. As systems that meet our vital national transportation interests for corporations' delivery trucks to deliver products, and grocer store chains to deliver food products for American citizens to purchase groceries in stores. These are just a few examples of how efforts within the transportation department, workers who build roads, and freeways enhance the quality of life for American citizens. Other existing organizations that work under the DOT title include the Federal Aviation Administration, the National Highway Traffic Safety Administration, the Federal Highway Administration, the Federal Transit Administration, the Federal Railroad Administration, and the Maritime Administration. The annual budget allocation for the Department OF Transportation is approximately $70 billion.

The Department OF Veterans Affairs looks after military soldiers, their families, through its' administering of healthcare, and other benefit programs for U.S. veterans or war survivors. Veterans Affairs became a part of the presidential cabinet in 1989. The type of benefit programs created by this departmental agency are pensions, education, disability compensation, home loans, life insurance, vocational rehabilitation, survivor support, medical care, and burial benefits with military honors. There are about 30 million veterans currently living, and nearly three of every four served during an official war or hostility conflict. Which is estimated to be about a quarter of our American population. Data from the Department OF Veterans Affairs details that there are about 72 million people who are potentially eligible for V.A. benefits and services. Due to the fact that they are veterans, or immediate family members, or spouse survivor of a veteran. The Secretary Of Veterans Affairs oversees the management of this agency by working closely with all armed forces branches of the U.S. military. While 235,000 employees conduct the day to day operations of this agency from work directives given from the secretary. The annual budget allocation for this vital cabinet department to function is $90 billion.

The Department OF The Treasury has the mission focus of attempting to secure the U.S. and international financial systems. The Secretary Of The Treasury manages this vital departmental component of our U.S. financial business system. Having regard for, operating with economic savvy, and maintenance of business finance systems with neighboring country partners. Attempting to oversee the financial infrastructure domestically, and internationally to safeguard vital parts of finance systems critical to American investment interests. This includes the production of coin, currency, disbursement of payments to the American public, the collection of taxes, and monetary loan borrowing of funds needed to run our federal government. The Treasury Department does work with other federal agencies, foreign governments, the international monetary fund, and international financial institutions of other nations. To encourage corporate development through investments, job creation, country industrialization, while encouraging global economic growth into financial business markets. Which in turn, over a long term raises the standard of living in the U.S., and globally. The overall work of this agency does also attempt to assist other nations prevent economic and financial crisis from plaguing its' citizens. The addition of computer technology, and internet has made it faster to do financial business around the world, but with that come cyber criminals. The Treasury Department now plays a critical role in improving technology base safeguards for our financial systems. This includes identifying the target support of corrupt financial networks as national security threats to catch criminals. While playing a role in implementing economic sanctions against countries seen as foreign threats, or are caught attempting to perpetrate a fraud on the American financial systems. This agency utilizes an employee staff of more than 100,000 to conduct the day to day business operations efficiently. The annual budget allocation for departmental operations is $13 billion.

The President Of The Executive Branch

There have been 45 acting Presidents Of The United States who were elected through ballot vote by the American people. To serve our country as both head of state in government, and as Commander-in-Chief of the various military branches of the armed forces. In every sense through the people or citizens, we all would like to have that natural inclination inside of us. That our United States President in his leadership and character permeates a feeling of a real presidential type stature. In a very vital time to this modern historical period of American history. Now the reigning executive commander-in- chief is faced with the responsibility of executing and enforcing all of the Laws created by the congress, and the 15 executive departments which are all now lead by members of the U.S. President's cabinet. To manage the administering and operations of our federal governments daily business. There are other existing agencies which operate within the executive branch, but are not part of the presidential cabinet. The Environmental Protection Agency, and the Central Intelligence Agency operate under the President Of The United States full ranking authority. The American president, through the executive branch operations also has the authority to appoint the administrative heads of more than 50 independent working federal commissions. Such as the leader of the Federal Reserve Board, the Securities and Exchange Commission, the appointment of Supreme Court federal judges, United States ambassadors, along with other federal governmental offices. The work of our American president is strategic, and plentiful in operational work task. That is why there are many applicable attorneys of Law, and other qualified business people in specified areas. Who work for the president to assist the operational management of our federal government. These people can be found in The Executive Office of the President. These employees are immediate staff available to the president. The U.S. President also appoints leadership in the Office Of Management and Budget, and the Office of the United States Trade Representative. The American president also has other major authoritative responsibilities like signing legislation produced by congress into Law or making the choice to veto bills enacted by U.S. congress. Although in some peculiar cases congress can override a presidential veto with a two-thirds vote. From both the House Of Representatives, and the Senate. Our nations president also engages in conducting diplomacy efforts with other nations, where serious American interests is a concern. In turn, the president has the authority to create negotiation of treaties and sign them into Law which also must be ratified by a Senate Two-thirds vote. In addition, the president can issue what are called executive order Laws without congress, and the President has unlimited power to extend pardons or clemencies for federal crimes. Except in cases of an imposed impeachment. Lastly, the American president has the legal Constitutional responsibility of delivering congress information of the State Of The Union. Which traditionally has taken place when joint sessions of congress are in during the month of January.

The Vice President

The Vice President of the United States major responsibility is to be ready at any moments notice. To take on the role of U.S. President if our current President becomes unable to perform his federal governmental work duty tasks. Instances that would permit such legal transfer of governmental political power. Are the current president's death, sudden resignation, temporary incapacitation, or if the majority of the cabinet and the Vice President make the judgment that the current president is no longer able to administer his operational duties as the American president. Another major role of the American Vice President is serving as the President of the United States Senate. In an instance where the Senate has voted on proposed referendum and there exist a tie in the vote, the Vice President would cast the deciding vote in such voting tie situations. Other governmental duties for the Vice President outside of those written in the text of the Constitution, are at the discretion of the American president. This government work may be specified policy, or simply serving as top adviser to the U.S. President. The Vice President works out of a business office in the West Wing of the White House, and has an office nearby in the Eisenhower Executive Office Building. There have been 48 acting Vice Presidents of the United States government. Of the 47 previous Vice Presidents that have served the American government, 9 have succeeded to the United States Presidency, and 4 have been elected as American President.

Chapter Four

Political Questions

Community Policing

Fair to say that there is a serious problem with some city police departments, and the police officers that are recruited to patrol our community streets in states cities across America. Demographics study and the type of crime association perpetrated by police officers, says the problem has become widespread across our country. Therefore, crime association can't necessarily be associated with a particular city community. However, a large number of crimes committed by police officers can be associated with crimes against a large number of black men. Which now has all of America asking questions. What is an efficient way to adequately create a legitimate way to do community policing without police officers committing crimes against citizens?

Community oriented policing is possible when public safety managers like the police chief of the police department possess a strategic plan for policing communities. A strategic plan which is thought out, then mapped out in detail for effective utilization by public safety managers along with police officers who will implement this plan. A prototype community oriented policing is a devised innovation in a cops' office. A strategic plan which makes community oriented policing possible always involves extensive study of the geographic area. That needs more assertive policing, plus crime data from these areas, information about the people who live in these community areas. Such as do they desire to have better public safety in their home community? Moreover, a police chief manager must take into account how many police officers will be needed to effectively implement a community-oriented policing plan. We must remember a policing plan is implementing policing behavior, so a police chief in their leadership style must have person to person relationships with their police officers. To have awareness of their police officers' personalities. We have read in our material resources that this is a somewhat useful tool to police chief managers to help predict behavior of employees, who implement job plans like community oriented policing. As we know people differ in terms of cognition, emotion, motivation, and ability. A police chief with person to person relationships with their officers strives to change this fact with strategic planning. To create a unified policing personality in police officers with behavior that is a complex function of a continuous interaction between the situation and the person. The situation is a developed person to person relationship with a police chief who possesses expert power intelligence in policing, and wants these police officers to implement a strategic community oriented policing plan with a unified interactional psychology work effort. The police officers are active players in the process, being changed by the created situation devised by the police chief, which allows them to be unified in cognition, emotion, motivation, and policing ability. Both the subjective view of the situation for officers, by the police chief, and the situation task of implementing an effective community oriented policing plan, are important to this process. After study of crime data within these communities' areas, and study of the people who live, conduct business, along with attend schools in these areas. The complete implementation of a highly effective community oriented policing plan is possible with the type of police officers illustrated. This practical building base is a step toward crime control in communities across America. Yes, these steps towards community oriented policing can be successful providing that police chief managers direct their mapped out plan effectively. By creating the right type of policing patrols in certain crime areas with effective law enforcement that either deters criminals from committing offenses, catches criminals in offending acts which lands them in jail, while creating community alliances with citizens of these communities that are being policed. To maintain within certain community norms and values that are already understood. So that citizens don't feel disenchantment with police services. This leads to successful community oriented policing with citizen involvement that allows for better crime control prevention. This creates a methodology as well for successful policing with a community oriented approach. On the reverse side it is not as feasible in a community whose interpersonal bonds are weak, nonexistent communication with police officers, or where fear has a high impact on citizens. Data on crime is not as forthcoming from citizens so reliance of data or information from on duty officer patrols is more relevant. However, doesn't always prove to be absolute, and at times a less interactive community alliance with police says that other citizens may be participating in illegal crime activity. So less communication with police officers within the community decreases the chance for crimes to be discovered. Some criminal justice social scientist may argue the applicability of my latter statement. Moreover, encountering such communities which differ in their alliance to public safety policing does make a police chief manager compare and contrast the choice of effective implementation of community policing plans. Does one stay with a community oriented policing plan in a neighborhood with citizen informant alliances, even if the crime rate has increased along with the nature of crimes. Or does one switch to a problem oriented plan in a community which is defined as emphasizing a more proactive policing after defining a heightened crime problem in certain hot zones of a community. Directed patrols at these areas, zero tolerance policies for criminal offenders who are caught in these areas. It is a fact that police chief managers study crime data, and the performance of police officers, this collected information is the determinant for chief managers of choice type of community patrols. Rather it be community oriented or problem oriented public safety policing. In hot zone crime areas effective problem oriented policing is utilized strategically to bring crime down in percentage. Yes, the community of people do have an affect on what type of public safety policing occurs within their community. Especially if they have a voice of concerns directed at officers, participate in criminal activity within their neighborhood, or create solid alliances with law enforcement officials to create crime control. The choice type of method to police communities most times is based on statistical crime data, and the amount of money allocated to implement public safety. This symbolizes the correlation association between the practice method of police, and policing funding. If I were a chief manager my implementation of community oriented policing would be in a community that has many citizen alliances like business owners, citizens who are informants about crimes, I could create police patrols in these areas to deter crime with less physical man power. While within certain community hot zones where crime rates are higher, and criminal activity does persist allow more police officers to spend a few more hours in these problem oriented areas. To be more proactive in policing to make arrest, and to deter other perspective criminal offenders, and to collect data on crime problems to effectively define crime in this area. With the hopes of effectively implementing a successful problem oriented policing plan for crime control and public safety. The advantages of my choice for both communities does allow me as a chief to allocate more police officer man power in certain crime ridden areas longer during work shifts. Creating more of a police presence in high crime areas, while still utilizing community oriented public safety policing in other communities. In researching past police relations initiatives, the United States Justice Department Attorney General Eric Holder has met with community citizens from problem oriented crime areas to discuss police misconduct, disenchantment with police services, to create community alliances with citizens of Albuquerque and Ferguson. To create better policing plans for these two cities and gain citizen trust in the police who provide public safety. Another such police relations initiative between policing officials and various members of the community is in Phoenix. They gather at Einstein's Bagels to have coffee and discuss community public safety efforts within a community that has a lot of homeless, and panhandlers. From the outside looking in the relation initiatives seem to be very positive in that the dialogue between the two groups exist, and is not a heated communication. In my opinion the steps that people who are officials are taking are for positive change in public safety along with law enforcement. The legal system could be better balanced or made better to improve relations with more police officers, judges, and attorneys from ethnic communities. The additional programs that could be added are public safety officials becoming monetary investors to create businesses in communities they serve. To create jobs for citizens. This could strengthen relationships between law enforcement officials and community folk. Lastly, police officers should also be required to be insured, so that if a crime is perpetrated by the officer, any restitution to victims would be paid from personal insurance. A way to make more cops a little more accountable while patrolling city communities. One has a tendency to think twice before pulling a trigger on a gun, if you have to flip a deductible or pay restitution personally.

The United States Of America in this 21st century has an increasing crime problem. Crimes associated with human aggression, criminal psychopathy, and mental disorders. Crime surge in the 1960's civil rights movement due to socio-economic oppression, and evil mistreatment of black Americans with Jim Crow laws. The surge in crime lasted through the 1970's war on crime spearheaded by president Richard Nixon. In this modern day the crimes being committed are offenses which range from minor traffic violations, DUI's, misdemeanor drug infractions within criminal justice courts, and an increasing number of violent criminal murders on our cities streets committed daily by law enforcement officers along with citizens. Police officers are increasingly involved in organized crime that create public safety hazards for U.S. citizens. Which as of late has become an increasing crime problem within the U.S., more than any other industrialized nation. As compared to other industrialized nations like China, who is said to have the second highest number of crime offenders incarcerated in the world at 1.5 million. The U.S. incarceration lock up rate for crime offenses is about 2.2 million the largest of any industrialized nation in the world. As a number statistic approximately 15, 209, 365 crimes are reported to the Federal Bureau Of Investigations in the United States each year. This increasing crime problem within the United States does alter or divert the lives of citizens who live in these states or local municipalities where these illustrated crimes do occur. Crime has become a political problem, a financial burden, and an increasingly social issue in public. Which creates a new psychology in other U.S. citizens throughout the country about crime, the people who are involved in committing crimes, how to protect themselves, and it creates a new human perception about the people in states or cities that have increasing crime rates.

Which in fact at times may divert some citizens who may be considered pillars of their community, because they contribute to keeping a community together or own a local business to move to other cities. Citizens move from crime infested, or effected environments due to their public safety concerns as a personal social issue. However, American media outlets do have a way of associating crimes to certain ethnic groups or communities. When data numbers express that crimes are committed by many existing racial groups. At any rate, as some businessmen, and citizens escape these crime environments the crimes themselves become a red alert to leading governmental public safety officials. As a question posed to them about what to do about crime to create public safety for communities, and citizens in public places. Moreover, creating a new public safety approach is defined as crime control. Expert power crime control is a reactive approach to crime problems. An political entities in states like municipal governmental public safety leading officials, and federal governmental people realize that defining crime environments along with criminal behavior is critically important. Critically important to regaining a grasp on crime within the United States, for public safety officials to create a new crime control. Through a methodological study of geographic environments within the United States where crimes are committed. Then as leading public safety officials creating a strategic effective management of policing crime plan, then implementing these new public safety plans to curtail crime for the good public safety of citizens. To create such a public safety plan with success these officials as I state study the definitions of crime being committed within specific geographic areas in the country. For example, in Phoenix, Arizona along with Oakland, California the crimes being committed and criminal offender profiles could be similar within this area of the country. Meaning that crimes could range from drug offenses with intent to sale, and the profile of the person committing the crime is a part of a group organization that sales drugs tagged as illegal by public safety officials who make laws. To further illustrate similar crime areas and offender profiles, the crime of murder is prevalent within certain year periods meaning that offenders are using handguns or rifles to kill their victims. An the offender is a part of another organized group defined in classification as a street gang. So public safety officials studying this geographic area can now examine this information and say with certainty that these crimes are similar, and the people committing the crimes have similar profile backgrounds of organized group affiliation. This is critically important to political entities because in the process of creating a new public safety plan that's effective, it must possess a strategic plan to curtail the crimes of drug sales along with murders but getting these groups off the streets as well by busting up their organization. So an effective management of an implemented crime control plan must deal with crime reduction, and people or groups as well. To further illustrate how public safety officials can study geographic crime areas but to see how crimes can differ without similarities, look at Beverly Hills, California. A white collar business area where most people have jobs, and is an upscale business area where citizens are well off monetarily. Crimes in these areas are more business oriented in that crimes occur within the management office of a business. A manager may be misappropriating money, or embezzling from the company because they are the leading official in charge of a company. So to implement a plan of effective crime control for public safety in this Beverly Hills area requires a different strategic plan. A plan of business nature which may include an audit of the business financial dealings which includes sales, bank accounts, and all pertinent documents including tax records. This is just to illustrate that when geographic crime areas in the United States are studied, public safety officials can then understand the crimes, define the crimes, define the type of criminal offending, then create a specific strategy for each crime environment. This is vital to creating a reactive approach to crime control, and as we have read in chapter one of course material readings, crimes do differ in certain areas. An local municipal public safety officials after studying crime areas, spend 50% of entire city budgets in states on strategic public safety plans. Moreover, the majority of money spent is on police officers, or staff implementing the public safety plan. This illustrates why understanding definitions of crime and criminal behavior are important to public safety officials who are seen as political entities as well. Moreover, crime is becoming an increasing problem within the United states but other industrialized countries as well. Which has become a financial burden for public safety officials to decide where to spend for crime control, a political football for politicians to use to make promises to citizens to stay in elected offices, but crime is an everyday social issue in public arenas which is constantly debated. To really put forth real ideas from American citizens for crime control remedy, which makes them feel safe in their community, and makes them feel safe in public while out conducting business or spending time with friends or family. I have illustrated answers for the posed questions to write this book, but there remains an existing dichotomy which continues to be exacerbated in American civilization about what citizens feel is effective management of crime control by leading public safety officials. Or are the public safety officials guilty of a crime themselves? This is what United States citizens continue to debate about those who are paid to protect the public.

Justice Courts

The role of the United States judicial system is to ensure the protection of civil rights of citizens along with rendering judicial review decisions of punitive punishment when crimes have occurred, or civil rights have been infringed. An overseeing the running of the government, and governmental department branches by maintaining adherence to the law. The laws of the U.S. constitution, state civil laws, and state criminal statutes. The United States judicial system carries out its define duties within U.S. courts overseeing cases which judicial power shall extend to all cases, in law and equity put before the court. To render decisions on cases which are called judicial reviews. Judicial reviews are the exercise of the courts power to decide cases and controversies after hearing a case between litigants. Which is exclusive judiciary power to broadly interpret the meaning of the constitution, state civil law, and state criminal statutes. All United States judicial system courts objective is to play this illustrated role within the parameters of the law. Moreover, no one court has all the responsibility and there is an existing judicial court separation of powers. So cases are put before the court for judicial reviews in local municipal courts, state county courts, state federal court, and the supreme court. No specific provision of the U.S. Constitution gives courts power to overturn the acts of elected branches of government within this illustration, as stated courts share legal roles. However, the supremacy clause is legally invoked by judges to strike down state or federal judicial reviews which are found to be unconstitutional. When inferior courts or lower courts fail to interpret the constitution correctly state supreme courts or the federal supreme court takes cases as final arbitrator. Making the attempt to define the scope of case information through justices' legal judicial power. Moreover, the role of the judicial system within criminal courts promotes public safety of country, and communities. With what is called a restorative justice philosophy. Which focuses on people who are victims of crime and the community. An restorative justice judicial courts create an interrelations process bringing people together victims, offenders, the community, and government. Where by cases are put before the court in states for judicial review, victims of crime can demand that offenders suffer punitive punishment, and psychological damage is repaired in victims of crimes when they are allowed to address criminal offenders in court. A creative judiciary process which ensures citizens civil rights, and public safety of communities across the country. Also, a process which nabs criminal offenders and incapacitates them to detention centers for punishment. It is clear that our current jury pools and court justices haven't been aligned with the views of the American people on some major crime cases presented to courts. Due to the fact that many American citizens feel that the judicial system has failed in many high profile murder cases, to hold suspected criminals accountable with guilty verdicts. Which has spawned a widespread distrust of our justice courts, and the feeling of many citizens in the American public is that our court system is not properly functioning.

Black People In America

Some of the most interesting to invent useful business products, and to innovate our American society with ingenuity are black people. Among some of the most beautiful people, and bright minds on the planet. Black folk have always possessed a recognizable talent that has always been useful to American society. As purpose driven people who are drivers of our industrialized civilization. However, the African-American in the United States remains a political question. About the real compensatory respect coming from government, respect from the police that patrol our community streets, and respect from other citizens in America. Regarding their legitimacy as real people, respect for their basic human rights in judicial courts as U.S. citizens, and being recognized as true pioneers of America. It's fair to say that my statements here are a large measure in totality of the past, current life, and culture for Afro-Americans in America. Yet, words that are a comprehensive conception of quality ideas that are accurate in interpreting the feelings that America communicates through its' loins to black people. It was black people at the center of the civil war conflict that caused many northern whites and southern whites to fight one another. And it was not until a close presidential election race, and the great compromise of 1877 partly spearheaded by congress members, that put black people back on plantations. An in effect caused whites of America to stop fighting each other over black folk. There is an existing dichotomy in that America had its first black president, whom many citizens that were not of color, and republicans made the attempt to repudiate his work efforts. Now the banner slogan of make America great again is being flown by a new president elect. As many American citizens not of color feel that America is now back to handling the business of the people. Yet, large numbers of African-Americans in this country are being innocently killed by police, and being denied justice in courts when it comes to the accused perpetrator of the crime. I am sure some scholars who study American criminal justice history would agree that America's old way of treatment towards black people is the new way. An if this is not the case, then it is time for states city governmental officials to work closely with the U.S. Justice Department to carefully and judiciously evaluate the black people question. To provide the entire black community the results from their work reflection, with a perspective on current crime trends that effect our community, and clarity on how we move forward. In turn, I urge people from the black community to inspire their children to want to be attorneys, judges, police officers, corrections detention officers, and public school teachers. Lastly, be vigilant as a community about illegal activity without taking the Law into your own hands. This includes illegal cop behavior on citizens, and even be willing to intervene to put a stop to it with deadly force. Especially when it's to protect an innocent person who hasn't committed a crime.

Chapter Five

Separation Of Powers Is Societal Segregation

It is our job as educational scholars to attempt to address human aggression, violence, and analyze the connection of these two terms to criminal behavior. Moreover, how these two illustrated terms create criminal behavior in American citizens. To be more specific I have chosen to address these topics by analyzing aggression and its connection to criminal behavior. Then create an opinion on why criminal behavior exist in our 21st century civilization based on documented facts. The topic of aggression is a serious issue because as it persists it causes violence. Aggression as it is seen by many United States citizens is proactive domination of people with aggressive military war conflicts, numerous public school shootings, and aggressive policing in urban communities. Which is felt to be unwarranted. Aggressive policing is seen as an increased police presence in communities which are urban with ethnic based racial make-ups with African-Americans, foreigners, and Mexican citizens where crime has not been data proven to be persistent. However, it is felt that without analyzing mathematical sample population crime data that this increased police presence is increased to persist to have a control over the citizen population in these areas.

By leading public safety policing leaders. What is seen as this proactive policing aggression utilizing domination of people with excessive force tactics to enforce municipal, and state legal statutes has caused suspected offenders to be harmed. Harmed physically causing bodily injuries, and in many instances being murdered when legal circumstances didn't warrant such police actions of aggression. This aggression has exposed criminal behavior being committed by public safety leading officials, and has contributed to citizens' social frustrations publicly about crimes. This public frustration about police crime coming directly from citizens is now a social risk factor which has spawned a persistence in criminal behavior. The citizens social learning about aggression has spawned violence throughout the country which has turned into criminal behavior. Citizens murdering police officers, and an alarming number of shooting attacks on public schools. While our federal government has increased its' insistence on war proliferation in other countries since 9/11. Moreover, this criminal behavior through violence from citizens, and war is a reactionary response with hot blooded forms of aggression. This reactive form of aggression is in response to 9/11, citizens being harmed by the police, and their complaints about police crime not being investigated or complaints found to be unwarranted. Moreover, this criminal behavior by what some criminal justice social scientist call two warring factions, has exacerbated social risk factors for the entire civilization at large for harm. Reactive aggressions as I have illustrated cause citizens to react through violence, riots which destroys communities, businesses, and harm people physically. It also increases crime among many people because there is a degree of anarchy when these reactions take place, people steal from businesses, guns are used, and property is destroyed. As I have illustrated aggression and its connection to criminal behavior, there is more to be said about the social risk factor among scientists with regard for the future of the United Sates. Moreover, how leaked news of aggression connected to criminal behaviors in this country is viewed internationally by American allies, and enemies. However, it's certainly clear that citizens are becoming more separated in society from one another. Due to their indifference to the management of government, and a large percentile base of citizens eligible to vote in at least presidential elections don't even participate in the electoral voting for political party candidates. The existing socio-economic living class which in most cases dictates where most people want to live. Has a type of effect on American citizens' participation in electing through vote, electing city officials, electing state officials, or potential candidates running for congress in our federal government. These are a few existing issues which has caused an emergence of the people of America's separation from politics, election voting, and staying informed about the management along with operations of local or federal governmental systems.

Before analyzing some of these previous statements with some legitimate facts, it's fair to say that many real citizens do envision an operable management of government. One form of federal governing within legal Constitutional boundaries, intricately connected to states, and city municipalities. Upholding a standard of serving "The People" of America, firm but fair in our judiciary system, and possessing congress men and women who consider all peoples values on issues which impact our country not just their party ideals. Before legally going to work to promote referendum into Laws. This is how many citizens feel government should work, and some have been misled thinking that our federal government does work this way. However, the true connection that many citizens feel they have to our government through their participation, the acts of congress, the types of bill referendum produced, and decisions in the judiciary assist citizens with forming new opinions. An often that connection to contributing to the operational functioning of our government the "The People" feel they have, becomes a disconnect or separational divide. This working process that has caused a divide among citizens, congress members, and judicial officials is simply from not seeing eye to eye. Which now many parts of our government and citizens are not together, and have lost their Aim&Purpose on what they envision as good government. That contributes to a productive government over long periods of time. Meanwhile, it's a given that life doesn't stop for politics to many citizens. Finding or having gainful job employment, possessing a car to travel to drop kids to day care, then making it to work just in the nick of time. Is how many Americans thriving in their day to day operations for earning monetarily, to possess a home to live in, as many nurture the development of their children within the place they call home, and even developing their own business life. However, the money that people earn from a job does dictate where, and how they can live. And in some situations it's a citizens working educational background that assist with obtaining more marketable employment with larger salaries. Often the larger salary wage earners in our society can dictate their own life circumstances better than a low hourly wage earning citizen. My latter statement, is often a vital reason that contributes to peoples' disconnection from participating in governmental systems or the political elections process. Their own life circumstances, often has many citizens consumed with their current situation only. Unworried about the direction of America, leaving that to other people among our states city population. Our current job employment economy has been significantly good for those citizens seriously looking for a job. However, often low wage work earning problems for citizens, and high percentage unemployment in ethnic communities that are not highly concentrated with adequate access to corporations that hire. Is the reality for many. A very large part of that existing constituency eligible to register to vote, do live mostly in these type of city communities around our country. Maybe what matters more to these citizens is working and wage earning. However, any person reading this book, or political science student reading this material that really has a vested interest in running for state local or federal office. Should be attempting to figure out how to galvanize people in these type of state city communities, to provide information that informs on how to change their current communities, and providing corporate resources in the form of jobs. To display a seriousness about getting people from these communities to re-connect a belief in American values, and believing in a political electoral process through voting. Which candidates that "The People" vote for, can produce results that American citizens need to truly change the scope of states city communities' direction. Through an increased standard of living in all areas of American citizens lives. Any good political scientists who has ambitions on running for governmental office, should definitely have this type of Aim&Purpose within the strategic framework of working for U.S. citizens or "The People". However, it is a realistic fact that no existing political party member in the states, or Washington, D.C. that we can think of, has been this type of candidate for the whole of American citizenry. I would argue that many of our citizens would envision this presentation of a prototype model of a candidate, as the ideal candidate that they would vote into a political office to represent their vested interests in America. However, the existing reality in the current facts about America's societal, and political arena dilemma is a display of separatism ideals. A people or citizenry that is not somehow intricately connected in agreement to the management, and day to day working operations of its' most vital governmental systems ultimately fails. Fails in the intended Aim& Purpose of the founding fathers vision for a United States. Without an inherent oneness carefully, and judicially arbitrated among citizens, and chosen political leaders there remains no existence of absolute power in that people. Which ultimately presents American society with what it has now, a separation of powers in a society which has become more segregated in its' opinionated views of America. An the complete functionality of our state and federal governmental systems as well. A real uniformity of power in the Aim&Purpose of citizens who are real people, and have an inherent care for their country are prolific in creating the project plans for building America. An the external view from citizens internationally of other countries who have the experience of seeing the building of such a country. Leave with a personal experience that one can reference, and creates foliage for a building tree within their own nation of origin. This is the type of uniformity in governmental power that sustains a lasting people. Not a uniformity of power in multiple acts of individual people who terrorize public school students with a gun, shoot up the work place, shoot fun seekers at country music concerts, shoot church goers, run people over in cars at a white supremacist rally, blow up a bomb at a marathon event, or just some crooked police officer who chooses to violate a citizens' civil rights while murdering the citizen in the process. An let us not forget that America has some of the best fighting military soldiers on the planet. Who have displayed a uniformity in power in fighting American enemies in other countries. Decimating the geographic landscape of these areas, the real people, and enemies that live there. Is America's uniformity in power only to be displayed through our military? Researchers that have tracked American history over the last 35 years would clearly argue that the U.S. is currently a much different country with a wide range of internal conflicts. While our country's military men & women have been engaged in war conflicts that have lasted currently more years than both world wars combined. It is inherently clear that our country is under tremendous pressure to find a solution to the separation of powers among the people of our society that has caused a large segregated gap between them because of separatist views. While citizens and governmental leadership fail to have any real interconnected American spirit, to arbitrate our country as being the cornerstone of a building process that effects billions of people around the globe. America was once a country that people around the world looked to in such a manner that express something very special about American values. An those very values expressed on Constitutional parchment paper are internalized by players on the political field because they are true Americans. It is the internal deterioration of a country from domestic conflicts, that cause people to rise and take a stance for something greater that they believe in. When they see a need for something called CHANGE. Simply, because they are American and want the very base ideals that their country was built upon to stand in principle on the political player battlefields they participate on. An in the everyday management, and operations of governmental political systems that many who are American still place a belief in the ideals. While in a gentle way not trying to politicize their own civil right in seeing the time for America to change, just acting on an inherent civil right given to American citizens. The very fact that human psychopathy in our society is a causation for human aggression, and is the existing risk factor for the many acts of unthinkable criminal behaviors in American society. That cause military war conflicts along with internal crime acts by citizens. May need more research and study of American citizens from a cultural psychological approach. Meanwhile, the separation of powers through people in intricate parts of our societal systems continues to unfold. In states local governments, in our federal governments political parties, within the judiciary, and even within our public entertainment industries like professional sports. That has truly effected the way that America operates as a country. There is a deep segregated divide in America among people who are real citizens, and there has to be a reconciliation of the problems facing our political government. In order for the people of America to devise innovative ways to re-invent a restructuring of our country's ideals. To build the country up from internal domestic conflicts, and military wars in order for future generations of American to have a prosperous future of progress. An to possess an inherent belief in the created structure of our working governmental political systems in America. That brings forth a galvanized change in states city communities people, who register to vote as participants in the process of electing life changing leadership into government office.

Separation of powers breeds societal segregation in congressional politics. Somehow, over generations it seems that our leadership in our nation's capital of Washington, D.C., have more so utilized political office as a lobby for specific interests' groups or corporations. Which often at times align with the membership of a particular political party. Business people with interests attempting to consult senate members about passing certain regulations, or promoting a specific type of referendum bill that better assist certain business investors along with their corporation. Which my explanations here is very opposite of what the founding fathers would see as real arbitration on issues that effect the whole of American citizenry, then legally bringing forth a helpful piece of referendum that is adequate for all the people. So it could definitely be arbitrarily argued that political party methodology matters more currently in congress, more so than the founding fathers' legal intentions. This is one issue proposed, but the fact is that even within political parties there is much disagreement on a lot of major societal issues which effect people and politicians. For example, there is a majority republican House Of Representatives along with a republican president. The issue of illegal immigration has been a hot topic for months throughout America, and in congress. Moreover, the citizens of this nation, democrats, and some republicans have been beckoning congress to devise a comprehensive immigration bill for the legislation to be signed into the Law by the president. Within the republican party a small framework of an immigration bill was started, then there were staunch disagreements among republicans. About further arbitrary facts to exclude, and specific legal text to include in this important bill framework. Ultimately, republicans couldn't agree on the bill or didn't want the legislation and now congress is on a stand still regarding a major issue in American society. Which on the external exclaims that the work for the people is not the priority. We the people must ask questions. What is the Aim&Purpose of the Senate?

A specific Aim&Purpose in politics or as a politician is having a strategic framework outlined. To meet the needs of American citizens, to innovate government so that its' operational functions are at the highest level, and ensuring the quality of expertise in every facet of governmental departments. So that our citizens can receive expedited services after thorough research of those services needed are arbitrarily considered by government employees. An then rendered to the people in a form that exclaims that our governmental systems are indeed working. It is a fact that major referendum issues before congress have been dragged out over a long period, issues related to black farmers, reparations for Afro-Americans, and now immigration. Every year it seems we hear about a government shut down due to indecisions among political parties about the budget to run the federal government. My point is that something major has occurred that has caused a segregated divide in politicians, and at a time in our American history where the condition of citizens in many states cities is very uncertain. Due to criminal acts of citizens and city leadership officials. It really seems that the divisions among people in our society have transformed our governmental systems into a downward spiral. An what has been lost is the specific

Aim&Purpose in a natural sense for governmental direction, and the strive of citizens' work progress that exclaims we can be a better America. Natural Aim&Purpose has a sense connection to any peoples' citizenry in any given nation. When citizens can connect with a oneness to that natural sense of a working Aim&Purpose, there seems to be a light vibrancy that resounds in the work to see future building. Rather if it's home construction building, building of corporations, or the building of a lasting governmental framework of systems that work for all the people. However, the natural sense of American Aim&Purpose seems to produce a different feeling from its' citizenry and leadership of a spreading chaos that needs to be grasped quickly. Simply, because the natural sense of Aim&Purpose has a connection to people who are citizens through their acts. Regardless if the people themselves feel connected or disconnected to this natural sense. This sense connection to the people even still of our world, has the power to dictate the future of America and its' people.

Let's switch gears for a moment to talk about the social politics of America. Many experts on civil society would agree that currently in the 21st Century American civilization, that socialism is a large part of U.S. citizens' life. Many congressional politicians who create American Governmental Laws often gather in socialist type events to raise money for campaigns, or to have discussions with their constituency. In their respective states about important issues in their community, or important politics discussions on their political party direction. Moreover, our society has many other realms for socialist type politics through media news like Fox News, MSNBC, CSPAN and other television networks specifically developed for mostly political discussions. At times multiple congressman appear on these networks to have news discussion panels about major political issues, and at times American citizens can call in on these shows over the phone to ask senators questions.

Another area of our American society which have a certain effect on politics in the American social arena are music entertainment. Many congressman, and even other employees of the Presidential cabinet love music. Often music entertainers are calendar booked to perform for leadership members of our government, and the public. Which at times does assist the political network among senators on opposing sides of referendum. To attempt to try to break divides among political parties to gain house votes in favor of proposed bills. In order for legal bills to be signed into Law by the President Of The United States. Other similar socialist events within our society that at times we see senators socializing at are NBA basketball games, NCAA basketball hoop games, MLB baseball games, NFL football games, NHL hockey games, or even appearing personally on late night television. This type of socialist politics is a way of sorts that engages senators with the public through entertainment. I can recall being at a High School track & field meet and seeing Senator Jeff Flake. However, senators do have other socialist type interests like a love for engineering, so you might see them visit a Chevy, Tesla, or Ford vehicle manufacturing plant. Or even attending the annual Library Of Congress book festival, due to their interests and like of books. There are often private parties that senators attend thrown by wealthy members of the American public as well. So I think it's fair to say that there is a lot of socialism in our current state of American politics. As a political education researcher, I strongly argue that American life in the 21st century is vastly public. In that computer internet technology, cable television, and even cell phones keep many American citizens engaged in social societal talk discussions. Even on politics. However, the fact remains that congress men & women when back on senate floors are judicially arbitrating referendum, still express a communicative sentiment far from what congress members no of the public. When this particular time in American history informs the people on every facet of our society, unlike any other time in American history. It is strongly believed that this sense of identifying with political party only, is spoiling the founding fathers' intent for congressional meetings. An the operational work management of our federal government at its' highest level. Not to say that this is all purposeful, but interpretive minds of political acts coming from our current executive branch could exclaim otherwise. To revert back in time into the socialist politics of congressional meetings in the 1770's, the sentiment among congress members did express a vital concern for America. A preservation of a country that was not already completely built, a socio-economic prosperity not already built, and even many citizens in the public were very keen on the direction of their country. Without other socialist type distractions. Although some opposing views may have been raised among popular congress members. There was always a point when a natural sense through the people would write legal history with a consensus effort. As stated, our current congress through the citizenry in America is expressing a communicative sentiment through acts in our society. Which are unmatched in frequency, while lasting effects of these acts conducted by our leadership and citizens have had more serious effects on all of America. In many ways that America may not be able to recover from or repair the damage done to the country. Yet, although many may be aware of these acts that effect our citizens, and political government. A political leadership complacency still looms over our nation's capital in Washington, D.C., and in states local city municipalities. While internal destruction of the country is clearly seen. As political science educational researchers, or students aspiring to work within the job employment field of politics. One must look at all the existing political issues, grasped their scientific complexity, then apply common sense, with application of specific solution anecdotes that are practical in nature. While creating a strategic network of qualified people with expertise that are willing to work within a method. To achieve societal goals for people who are citizens, and governmental leadership goals as well. Your personal role as a worker may be to register thousands of election voters, but understanding the effect that one can have by taking part as an active political player. Potentially impacts the leadership of America, and the impression impact that our country's politics has on the entire world.

www.ingramcontent.com/pod-product-compliance
Lightning Source LLC
Chambersburg PA
CBHW072257260726

48658CB00001BA/496